Virtues

of

Courage in Adversity

WILLIAM J. BENNETT

W PUBLISHING GROUP™

www.wpublishinggroup.com

A Division of Thomas Nelson, Inc.
www.ThomasNelson.com

Published by W Publishing Group, a Division of Thomas Nelson, Inc., P.O. Box 141000, Nashville,
Tennessee 37214.

Material in this book is compiled from both *The Book of Virtues* and *The Moral Compass* by William
J. Bennett, copyright © 1993 by William J. Bennett and copyright © 1996 by William J. Bennett.

Published by arrangement with Simon & Schuster, Inc.

Library of Congress Cataloging-in-Publication Data

Virtues of courage in adversity / [edited by] William J. Bennett.
    p. cm.
  ISBN 0–8499–1724–7
   1. Courage—Literary collections. I. Bennett, William J. (William John), 1943–
PN6071.C815 V57 2002
808.8'0353—dc21   2001046980

Printed in the United States of America

01 02 03 04 05 BVG 5 4 3 2 1

Contents

Introduction

WILLIAM J. BENNETT

L ook at a man in the midst of doubt and danger, and you will learn in his hour of adversity what he really is," wrote the Roman philosopher Lucretius. "It is then that true utterances are wrung from the recesses of his breast. The mask is torn off; the reality remains."

Some people's lives see more hardship than others. But make no mistake—every life's journey has some tough stretches. Everyone is tested, everyone brought to the line. There will be occasional bumps in the road, unpleasant surprises, irritating delays, annoying mistakes and accidents. There will be days when everything seems to go wrong, and moments when our whole world seems to be falling apart. Adversity is a part of every life. "Man is born unto trouble, as the sparks fly upward," the book of Job reminds us.

Courage is one of the foremost virtues we use to meet adversity. In this book, we meet some people who put courage to good use, sometimes in moments of crisis. Here we find people standing firm at their posts and sticking to their assignments, even though temptation may beckon them away. We witness people winning by small steps. We learn a few things about facing bleak situations, ones in which dangers of pain and loss lie ahead.

The virtue of courage needs practical wisdom as a guide. You have to be able to recognize *when* the time is right to fight, and then you have to know *how* to get through those tough times. The selections in this book help sharpen our intellectual virtues as well as our moral ones. We meet examples of reason giving direction to action. We learn the value of ingenuity in tough spots and fortitude under heavy fire. We see real concentration in action, a harnessing of thought and talent that brings the whole mind and whole heart to a task. And we witness the courage of imagination, the kind that dares to stick up for worthy ideas when everyone else shouts they're wrong.

If met correctly, of course, most of the troubles we encounter become opportunities to lead fuller, better lives. The blows of adversity can be the best chances for improvement. "The gem cannot be polished without friction," a Chinese proverb says. Any real achievement, any worthwhile prize, will come at the cost of a few failures.

There are places we can look for courage as we struggle through tough times. The best source, as David found when he faced Goliath, is faith. "Be of good courage, and he shall strengthen your heart, all ye that hope in the Lord," the book of Psalms exhorts. In the end, faith in God is the surest master of fear.

Courage in adversity is half the battle, but it does not always win the battle. Sometimes things don't turn out quite the way we hoped. In those times we must trust that the struggle itself was worth it, remembering that we are measured by how we conducted ourselves along the way. Then we must ready ourselves for new tests knowing, as the clergyman Henry Ward Beecher put it more than one hundred years ago, "We are always in the forge, or on the anvil; by trials God is shaping us for higher things."

An Appeal from the Alamo

WILLIAM BARRET TRAVIS

*The Alamo in San Antonio, Texas, has become an American sym-
bol of unyielding courage and self-sacrifice. A force of Texans captured
the mission fort in late 1835 after the outbreak of revolution against
the dictatorship of Mexican General Antonio López de Santa Anna.
By early 1836, Lieutenant Colonel William Barret Travis and the
fort's garrison found themselves hemmed in by a Mexican army swelling
to six thousand troops. On February 24, Travis dispatched couriers to
nearby Texas towns, carrying frantic appeals for aid. Fewer than three
dozen men picked their way through enemy lines to join the Alamo's
defenders. The siege continued until March 6, when Santa Anna's
forces overwhelmed the fort. The entire garrison was killed, some 180
men, including Colonel Travis, James Bowie, and Davy Crockett.*

Commandancy of the Alamo, Texas
February 24, 1836

To the People of Texas and All Americans in the World.
Fellow Citizens and Compatriots:

I am besieged by a thousand or more of the Mexicans under
Santa Anna. I have sustained a continual bombardment and can-
nonade for twenty-four hours and have not lost a man. The
enemy has demanded a surrender at discretion; otherwise, the
garrison are to be put to the sword if the fort is taken. I have
answered the demand with a cannon shot, and our flag still
waves proudly from the walls. *I shall never surrender nor retreat.*
Then, I call on you in the name of Liberty, of patriotism, and of
everything dear to the American character, to come to our aid
with all dispatch. The enemy is receiving reinforcements daily
and will no doubt increase to three or four thousand in four or
five days. If this call is neglected, I am determined to sustain
myself as long as possible and die like a soldier who never forgets
what is due to his own honor and that of his country.

VICTORY OR DEATH.
William Barret Travis
Lieutenant Colonel,
Commandant

The Brave Three Hundred

ADAPTED FROM JAMES BALDWIN

The famous battle at the narrow Pass of Thermopylae took place in 480 B.C., when Xerxes led a Persian army into Greece. Even though they were defeated at Thermopylae, the Spartans' heroic stand against overwhelming odds inspired the Greeks in later resistance and forever made Sparta's name synonymous with courage.

All of Greece was in danger. A mighty army, led by Xerxes, the great king of Persia, had come from the east. It was marching along the seashore, and in a few days would be in Greece. Xerxes had sent messengers into every city and state, demanding that they send him water and earth as symbols that the land and the sea were his. The Greeks refused, and resolved to defend their freedom against the invaders.

And so there was a great stir throughout all the land. The Greeks armed themselves and hurried to go out and drive back their foe.

There was only one way by which the Persian army could go into Greece on that side, and that was through a narrow pass between the mountains and the sea. It was called the pass at Thermopylae, a word which meant "hot gates" because of the hot springs nearby.

This pass was guarded by Leonidas, the king of the Spartans, with only a few thousand troops. They were greatly outnumbered by the Persian army, but they felt confident. They had positioned themselves in the narrowest part of the pass, where a few men armed with long spears could hold back an entire company.

The first Persian wave of attack started toward the pass at dawn. The Spartan scouts reported that there were so many troops, their arrows would darken the sun like a cloud.

"So much the better," Leonidas said. "We can fight better in the shade."

The arrows came down, but the Greeks' shields deflected them, and their long spears held back the Persians who pressed into the pass. The invaders attacked again and again, but each time they were repulsed with terrible losses. At last Xerxes sent forward his best troops, known as the Ten Thousand Immortals, but even they fared no better against the determined Greeks.

After two days of attacks, Leonidas still held the pass. But that night a man was brought to Xerxes' camp. He was a Greek who knew the local terrain well, and he was ready to sell a secret: the pass was not the only way through. A hunters' footpath wound the long way around, to a trail along the spine of the mountain. It was held by only a handful of Greeks. They could be easily routed, and then Xerxes could attack the Spartan army from the rear.

The treacherous plan worked. The men guarding the secret trail were surprised and beaten. A few managed to escape in time to warn Leonidas.

The Greeks knew that if they did not abandon the pass at once, they would be trapped. But Leonidas also knew he must delay Xerxes longer while the Greek cities prepared their defenses. He made his decision. He ordered almost all of his troops to slip through the mountains and back to their cities, where they would be needed. He kept his royal guard of three hundred Spartans as well as a few other troops, and prepared to defend the pass to the end.

Xerxes and his army came forward. The Spartans stood fast, but one by one they fell. When their spears broke, they stood side by side, fighting with swords or daggers or only their fists.

All day long they kept the Persian army at bay. But when the sun went down, there was not one Spartan left alive. Where they had stood was only a heap of the slain, all bristled over with spears and arrows.

Xerxes had taken the pass, but at a cost of thousands of men and a delay of several days. The time cost him dearly. The Greek navy was able to gather its forces, and soon afterward it managed to drive Xerxes back to Asia.

Many years later a monument was erected at the pass of Thermopylae, inscribed in memory of the courageous stand of a few in defense of their homeland:

> *Pause, traveler, ere you go your way. Then tell*
> *How, Spartan to the last, we fought and fell.*

Chanticleer and Partlet

RETOLD BY J. BERG ESENWEIN AND
MARIETTA STOCKARD

This story comes from the "Nun's Priest's Tale," one of Chaucer's
Canterbury Tales. *It reminds us that there is such a thing as false
courage, which may rise from our own vanity. There are some dangers
we should rightly fear, and we shouldn't be embarrassed about a proper
wariness of them.*

Once there was a barnyard close to a wood, in a little valley. Here dwelt a cock, Chanticleer by name. His comb
was redder than coral, his feathers were like burnished gold,
and his voice was wonderful to hear. Long before dawn each
morning his crowing sounded over the valley, and his seven
wives listened in admiration.

One night as he sat on the perch by the side of Dame Partlet,
his most loved mate, he began to make a curious noise in his
throat.

"What is it, my dear?" said Dame Partlet. "You sound frightened."

"Oh!" said Chanticleer, "I had the most horrible dream. I thought that as I roamed down by the wood a beast like a dog sprang out and seized me. His color was red, his nose was small, and his eyes were like coals of fire. Ugh! It was fearful!"

"Tut, tut! Are you a coward to be frightened by a dream? You've been eating more than was good for you. I wish my husband to be wise and brave if he would keep my love!" Dame Partlet clucked, as she smoothed her feathers, and slowly closed her scarlet eyes. She felt disgusted at having her sleep disturbed.

"Of course you are right, my love, yet I have heard of many dreams which came true. I am sure I shall meet with some misfortune, but we will not talk of it now. I am quite happy to be here by your side. You are very beautiful, my dear!"

Dame Partlet unclosed one eye slowly and made a pleased sound, deep in her throat.

The next morning, Chanticleer flew down from the perch and called his hens about him for their breakfast. He walked about boldly, calling, "Chuck! Chuck!" at each grain of corn which he found. He felt very proud as they all looked at him so admiringly. He strutted about in the sunlight, flapping his wings to show off his feathers, and now and then throwing back his head and crowing exultantly. His dream was forgotten; there was no fear in his heart.

Now all this time, Reynard, the fox, was lying hidden in the bushes on the edge of the wood bordering the barnyard. Chanticleer walked nearer and nearer his hiding place. Suddenly he saw a butterfly in the grass, and as he stooped toward it, he spied the fox.

"Cok! Cok!" he cried in terror, and turned to flee.

"Dear friend, why do you go?" said Reynard in his gentlest voice. "I only crept down here to hear you sing. Your voice is like an angel's. Your father and mother once visited my house. I should so love to see you there, too. I wonder if you remember your father's singing? I can see him now as he stood on tiptoe, stretching out his long slender neck, sending out his glorious voice. He always flapped his wings and closed his eyes before he sang. Do you do it in the same way? Won't you sing just once and let me hear you? I am so anxious to know if you really sing better than your father."

Chanticleer was so pleased with this flattery that he flapped his wings, stood up on tiptoe, shut his eyes and crowed as loudly as he could.

No sooner had he begun then Reynard sprang forward, caught him by the throat, threw him over his shoulder, and made off toward his den in the woods.

The hens made a loud outcry when they saw Chanticleer being carried off, so that the people in the cottage nearby heard and ran out after the fox. The dog heard and ran yelping after him. The cow ran, the calf ran, the pigs began to squeal and run, too. The ducks and geese quacked in terror and flew up into the treetops. Never was there heard such an uproar. Reynard began to feel a bit frightened himself.

"How swiftly you do run!" said Chanticleer from his back. "If I were you I should have some sport out of those slow fellows who are trying to catch you. Call out to them and say, 'Why do you creep along like snails? Look! I am far ahead of you and shall soon be feasting on this cock in spite of all of you!'"

Reynard was pleased at this and opened his mouth to call to his pursuers; but as soon as he did so, the cock flew away from him and perched up in a tree safely out of reach.

The fox saw he had lost his prey and began his old tricks again. "I was only proving to you how important you are in the barnyard. See what a commotion we caused! I did not mean to frighten you. Come down now and we will go along together to my home. I have something very interesting to show you there."

"No, no," said Chanticleer. "You will not catch me again. A man who shuts his eyes when he ought to be looking deserves to lose his sight entirely."

By this time, Chanticleer's friends were drawing near, so Reynard turned to flee. "The man who talks when he should be silent deserves to lose what he has gained," he said as he sped away through the wood.

Courage

JOHN GALSWORTHY

Here is the kind of bravery that shoulders another's misfortunes. John Galsworthy (1867–1933) has depicted a particularly dramatic example, but if we look around we'll see the same strong-hearted courage in teachers, ministers, policemen, and others who spend whole lives coming to the rescue.

At that time (said Ferrand) I was in poverty. Not the kind of poverty that goes without dinner, but the sort that goes without breakfast, lunch, and dinner, and exists as it can on bread and tobacco. I lived in one of those fourpenny lodging houses, Westminster way. Three, five, seven beds in a room; if you pay regularly, you keep your own bed; if not, they put someone else there who will certainly leave you a memento of himself. It's not the foreigners' quarter; they are nearly all English, and drunkards. Three quarters of them don't eat—can't; they have no capacity for solid food. They drink and drink. They're not worth wasting your

10

money on—cabrunners, newspaper boys, sellers of laces, and what you call sandwich men; three fourths of them brutalized beyond the power of recovery. What can you expect? They just live to scrape enough together to keep their souls in their bodies; they have no time or strength to think of anything but that. They come back at night and fall asleep—and how dead that sleep is! No, they never eat—just a bit of bread; the rest is drink!

There used to come to that house a little Frenchman, with a yellow crow's-footed face; not old either, about thirty. But his life had been hard—no one comes to these houses if life is soft, especially no Frenchman; a Frenchman hates to leave his country. He came to shave us—charged a penny; most of us forgot to pay him, so that in all he shaved about three for a penny. He went to others of these houses—this gave him his income—he kept the little shop next door, too, but he never sold anything. How he worked! He also went to one of your Public Institutions; this was not so profitable, for there he was paid a penny for ten shaves. He used to say to me, moving his tired fingers like little yellow sticks: "Pff! I slave! To gain a penny, friend, I'm spending fourpence. What would you have? One must nourish oneself to have the strength to shave ten people for a penny." He was like an ant, running round and round in his little hole, without any chance but just to live; and always in hopes of saving enough to take him back to France, and set him up there. We had a liking for each other. He was the only one, in fact—except a sandwich-man who had been an actor, and was very intelligent, when he wasn't drunk—the only one in all that warren who had ideas. He was fond of pleasure and loved his music hall—must have gone at least twice a year, and was always talking of it. He had little knowledge of its joys, it's true—hadn't the money for that—but his intentions were good. He used to keep me till the last, and shave me slowly.

"This rests me," he would say. It was amusement for me, too, for I had got into the habit of going for days without opening my lips. It's only a man here and there one can talk with; the rest only laugh. You seem to them a fool, a freak—something that should be put into a cage or tied by the leg.

"Yes," the little man would say, "when I came here first I thought I should soon go back, but now I'm not so sure. I'm losing my illusions. Money has wings, but it's not to *me* it flies. Believe me, friend, I am shaving my soul into these specimens. And how unhappy they are, poor creatures; how they must suffer! Drink! You say. Yes, that saves them—they get a little happiness from that. Unfortunately, I haven't the constitution for it—here." And he would show me where he had no constitution. "You, too, comrade, you don't seem to be in luck; but then, you're young. Ah, well, *faut eaftre philosophe*—but imagine what kind of a game it is in this climate, especially if you come from the South!"

When I went away, which was as soon as I had nothing left to pawn, he gave me money—there's no question of lending in those houses: if a man parts with money he *gives* it, and lucky if he's not robbed into the bargain. There are fellows there who watch for a new pair of shoes, or a good overcoat, profit by their wakefulness as soon as the other is asleep, and promptly disappear. There's no morality in the face of destitution—it needs a man of iron, and these are men of straw. But one thing I will say of the low English—they are not bloodthirsty, like the low French and Italians.

Well, I got a job as fireman on a steamer, made a tour tramping, and six months later I was back again. The first morning I saw the Frenchman. It was shaving day. He was more like an ant than ever, working away with all his legs and arms; a little yellower, and perhaps more wrinkled.

"Ah!" he called out to me in French, "there you are—back again. I knew you'd come. Wait till I've finished with this specimen—I've a lot to talk about."

We went into the kitchen—a big stone-floored room, with tables for eating—and sat down by the fire. It was January, but, summer or winter, there's always a fire burning in that kitchen.

"So," he said, "you have come back? No luck? Eh! Patience! A few more days won't kill you at your age. What fogs, though! You see, I'm still here, but my comrade, Pigon, is dead. You remember him—the big man with black hair who had the shop down the street. Amiable fellow, good friend to me, and married. Fine woman his wife—a little ripe, seeing she has had children, but of good family. He died suddenly of heart disease. Wait a bit; I'll tell you about that. . . .

"It was not long after you went away, one fine day in October, when I had just finished with these specimens here, and was taking my coffee in the shop, and thinking of that poor Pigon—dead then just three days—when *pom!* comes a knock, and there is Madame Pigon! Very calm—a woman of good family, well brought up, well made—fine woman. But the cheeks pale, and the eyes so red, poor soul.

"'Well, Madame,' I asked her, 'what can I do for you?'

"It seems this poor Pigon died bankrupt; there was not a cent in the shop. He was two days in his grave, and the bailiffs in already.

"'Ah, Monsieur!' she says to me, 'what am I to do?'

"'Wait a bit, Madame!' I get my hat and go back to the shop with her.

"What a scene! Two bailiffs, who would have been the better for a shave, sitting in a shop before the basins; and everywhere, *ma foi,* everywhere, children! Tk! Tk! A little girl of ten, very like her mother; two little boys with little trousers, and one with nothing but a chemise; and others—two, quite small, all rolling on the floor. And what a horrible noise!—all crying, all but the little girl, fit to break themselves in two. The bailiffs seemed perplexed. It was enough to make one weep! Seven! And some quite small! That poor Pigon, I had no idea!

"The bailiffs behaved very well.

"'Well,' said the biggest, 'you can have four-and-twenty hours to find this money; my mate can camp out here in the shop—we don't want to be hard on you!'

"I helped Madame to soothe the children.

"'If I had the money,' I said, 'it should be at your service, Madame—in each well-born heart there should exist humanity; but I have no money. Try and think whether you have no friends to help you.'

"'Monsieur,' she answered, 'I have none. Have I had time to make friends—I, with seven children?'

"'But in France, Madame?'

"'None, Monsieur. I have quarreled with my family; and

reflect—it is now seven years since we came to England, and then only because no one would help us.'

"That seemed to me bad, but what could I do? I could only say, 'Hope always, Madame—trust in me!'

"I went away. All day long I thought how calm she was—magnificent! And I kept saying to myself: 'Come, tap your head! Tap your head! Something must be done!' But nothing came.

"The next morning it was my day to go to that sacred Institution, and I started off still thinking what on earth could be done for the poor woman. It was as if the little ones had got hold of my legs and were dragging at me. I arrived late, and, to make up time, I shaved them as I have never shaved them; a hot morning—I perspired! Ten for a penny! Ten for a penny! I thought of that, and of the poor woman. At last I finished and sat down. I thought to myself: 'It's too strong! Why do you do it? It's stupid! You are wasting yourself!' And then, my idea came to me! I asked for the manager.

"'Monsieur,' I said, 'it is impossible for me to come here again.'

"'What do you mean?' says he.

"'I have had enough of your—"ten for a penny"—I am going to get married. I can't afford to come here any longer. I lose too much flesh for the money.'

"'What!' he says, 'you're a lucky man if you can afford to throw away your money like this!'

"'Throw away my money! Pardon, Monsieur, but look at me'—I was still very hot—'for every penny I make I lose three-pence, not counting the boot leather to and fro. While I was still a bachelor, Monsieur, it was my own affair—I could afford these extravagances. But now—it must finish—I have the honor, Monsieur!'

"I left him, and walked away. I went to the Pigons' shop. The bailiff was still there—Pfui! He must have been smoking all the time.

"'I can't give them much longer,' he said to me.

"'It is of no importance,' I replied, and I knocked, and went into the back room.

"The children were playing in the corner, that little girl, a heart of gold, watching them like a mother; and Madame at the table with a pair of old black gloves on her hands. My friend, I have never seen such a face—calm, but so pale, so frightfully discouraged, so overwhelmed. One would say she was waiting for her death. It was bad, it was bad—with the winter coming on!

"'Good morning, Madame,' I said. 'What news? Have you been able to arrange anything?'

"'No, Monsieur. And you?'

"'No!' And I looked at her again—a fine woman; ah! A fine woman.

"'But,' I said, 'an idea has come to me this morning. Now, what would you say if I asked you to marry me? It might possibly be better than nothing.'

"She regarded me with her black eyes, and answered, 'But willingly, Monsieur!' And then, comrade, but not till then, she cried."

The little Frenchman stopped and stared at me hard.

"H'm!" I said at last, "you have courage!"

He looked at me again; his eyes were troubled, as if I had paid him a bad compliment.

"You think so?" he said at last, and I saw that the thought was gnawing at him, as if I had turned the light on some desperate, dark feeling in his heart.

"Yes!" he said, taking his time, while his good yellow face wrinkled and wrinkled, and each wrinkle seemed to darken. "I was afraid of it even when I did it. Seven children!" Once more he looked at me. "And since!—sometimes—sometimes—I could—" He broke off, then burst out again.

"Life is hard! What would you have? I knew her husband. Could I leave her to the streets?"

The Crisis

THOMAS PAINE

These famous words by Thomas Paine appeared during the winter of 1776–1777, a time that may have been the gloomiest hour for the American revolutionary cause. The patriot forces seemed unable to win a battle. George Washington's army had been routed out of New York, driven across New Jersey, and lay shivering on the Pennsylvania side of the Delaware River. More and more men deserted every day. Racked by hunger, cold, and disease, those who remained simply waited in misery for their enlistments to expire so they could go home. Washington himself confided in a letter to a relative: "I think the game is pretty near up." Amid this crisis of morale, Paine implored the colonists not to give up the fight.

These are the times that try men's souls. The summer soldier and the sunshine patriot will, in this crisis, shrink from the service of their country; but he that stands it now, deserves the love and thanks of man and woman. Tyranny, like hell, is not easily conquered; yet we have this consolation with us, that the harder the conflict, the more glorious the triumph. What we obtain too cheap, we esteem too lightly: it is dearness only that gives every thing its value. Heaven knows how to put a proper price upon its goods; and it would be strange indeed if so celestial an article as FREEDOM should not be highly rated. . . .

I call not upon a few, but upon all: not on *this* state or *that* state, but on *every* state: up and help us; lay your shoulders to the wheel; better have too much force than too little, when so great an object is at stake. Let it be told to the future world, that in the depth of winter, when nothing but hope and virtue could survive, that the city and the country, alarmed at one common danger, came forth to meet and to repulse it. Say not that thousands are gone, turn out your tens of thousands; throw not the burden of the day upon Providence, but *"show your faith by your works,"* that God may bless you. It matters not where you live, or what rank of life you hold, the evil or the blessing will reach you all. The far and the near, the home counties and the back, the rich and the poor, will suffer or rejoice alike. The heart that feels not now, is dead: the blood of his children will curse his cowardice, who shrinks back at a time when a little might have saved the whole, and made *them* happy. I love the man that can smile in trouble, that can gather strength from distress, and grow brave by reflection. 'Tis the business of little minds to shrink; but he whose heart is firm, and whose conscience approves his conduct, will pursue his principles unto death.

Crossing the Rubicon

ADAPTED FROM JAMES BALDWIN

By law, Roman magistrates could bring armies into Italy only by permission of the Senate. By marching his legions across the Rubicon in 49 B.C., Julius Caesar committed himself to a showdown with Rome itself.

Rome was the most powerful city in the world. The Romans had conquered all the countries on the north side of the Mediterranean Sea and most of those on the south side. They also occupied the islands of the sea and all that part of Asia that now belongs to Turkey.

Julius Caesar had become the hero of Rome. He had led a large army into Gaul, that part of Europe which today includes France, Belgium, and Switzerland, and turned it into a Roman province. He had crossed the Rhine and subdued a part of Germany. Caesar's army even went into Britain, a wild and remote country to the Romans, and established colonies there.

For nine years Caesar and his army had served Rome loyally

and well. But Caesar had many enemies at home, people who feared his ambitions and envied his accomplishments, people who cringed every time they heard Caesar called a great hero.

One of these persons was Pompey, who had long been the most powerful man in Rome. Like Caesar, he was the commander of a great army, but his troops had done very little to win the applause of the people. Pompey saw that, unless something occurred to prevent it, Caesar would in time be his master. He therefore began to lay plans to destroy him.

In another year the time of Caesar's service in Gaul would end. It was understood that he would then return home and be elected consul, or ruler, of the mighty Roman republic. He would then be the most powerful man in the world.

Pompey and other enemies of Caesar were determined to prevent this. They induced the Roman Senate to send a command to Caesar to leave his army in Gaul and come at once to Rome. "If you do not obey this command," said the Senate, "you shall be considered an enemy to the republic."

Caesar knew what that meant. If he went to Rome alone, his enemies would make false accusations against him. They would try him for treason and keep him from being elected consul.

He called the soldiers of his favorite legion together and told them about the plot that had been made for his ruin. The veterans who had followed him through so many perils, and had helped him win so many victories, declared they would not leave him. They would go with him to Rome and see that he received his due rewards. They would serve without pay, and even share the expenses of the long march.

The troops started toward Italy with flags flying. The soldiers were even more enthusiastic than Caesar himself. They climbed mountains, waded rivers, endured fatigue, faced all kinds of dangers for the sake of their leader.

At last they came to a little river called the Rubicon. It was the boundary line of Caesar's province of Gaul; on the other side lay Italy. Caesar paused a moment on the bank.

He knew that to cross the stream would be to declare war against Pompey and the Roman Senate. It might involve all Rome in a fearful strife, the end of which no man could foresee.

"We could still go back," he told himself. "Behind us lies safety. But once we cross the Rubicon into Italy, turning around is impossible. I must make the choice here."

He did not hesitate long. He gave the word and rode boldly across the shallow stream.

"We have crossed the Rubicon!" he cried as he reached the far shore. "There is no turning back."

The news was shouted along the roads and byways leading to Rome: Caesar had crossed the Rubicon! People from every town and village turned out to welcome the returning hero as he marched through the countryside. The closer he drew to Rome, the wilder people celebrated his arrival. Finally Caesar and his army reached the gates of the city. No troops came out to challenge them, and there was no resistance when Caesar marched into the city itself. Pompey and his allies had fled.

For more than two thousand years, men and women facing daring decisions have thought of Caesar at the edge of the stream before they too crossed their Rubicons.

David and Goliath

RETOLD BY J. BERG ESENWEIN AND
MARIETTA STOCKARD

This story has it all: the dauntless courage of youth, the thrill of a terrible giant, the overthrowing of a seemingly invincible warrior by means of a mere child's weapon, and a hero who wins through the strength of his faith.

Long ago, in the land of Bethlehem, there lived a man named Jesse, who had eight stalwart sons. The youngest of these sons was David.

Even as a little lad, David was ruddy, beautiful of countenance, and strong of body. When his older brothers drove the flocks to the fields, he ran with them. Each day as he leaped over the hillsides, listened to the gurgling water in the brooks, and the songs of birds in the trees, he grew stronger of limb, and more filled with joy and courage. Sometimes he made songs of the beautiful things he saw and heard. His eye was keen, his hands strong, and his aim sure. When he fitted a stone into his sling, he never missed the mark at which he threw it.

As he grew older, he was given the care of a part of the flocks. One day as he lay on the hillside keeping watch over his sheep, a lion rushed out of the woods and seized a lamb. David leaped to his feet and ran forward. He had no fear in his heart, no thought but to save the lamb. He sprang upon the lion, seized him by his hairy head, and with no weapon but the staff in his strong young hands, he slew him. Another day, a bear came down upon them. Him also, David slew.

Now, soon after this, the Philistines marshaled their armies and came across the hills to drive the children of Israel away from their homes. King Saul gathered his armies and went out to meet them. David's three oldest brothers went with the king, but David was left at home to tend the sheep. "Thou art too young; stay in the fields and keep the flocks safe," they said to David.

Forty days went by, and no news of the battle came; so Jesse called David to him and said: "Take this food for thy brethren, and go up to the camp to see how they fare."

David set out early in the morning, and journeyed up to the hill on which the army was encamped. There was great shouting and the armies were drawn up in battle array when David arrived. He made his way through the ranks and found his brethren. As he stood talking with them, silence fell upon King Saul's army; and there on the hillside opposite stood a great giant. He strode up and down, his armor glittering in the sun. His shield was so heavy that the strongest man in King Saul's army could not have lifted it, and the sword at his side was so great that the strongest arm could not have wielded it.

"It is the great giant, Goliath," David's brethren told him. "Each day he strides over the hill and calls out his challenge to the men of Israel, but no man amongst us dares to stand before him."

"What! Are the men of Israel afraid?" asked David. "Will they let this Philistine defy the armies of the living God? Will no one go forth to meet him?" He turned from one to another, questioning them.

Eliab, David's oldest brother, heard him and was angry. "Thou art naughty and proud of heart," he said. "Thou hast stolen away from home thinking to see a great battle. With whom hast thou left the sheep?"

"The keeper hath charge of them; and our father, Jesse, sent me hither; and my heart is glad that I am come," answered David. "I myself will go forth to meet this giant. The God of Israel will go with me, for I have no fear of Goliath nor of all his hosts!"

The men standing near hastened to the tent of King Saul and told him of David's words.

"Let him stand before me," commanded the king.

When David was brought into his presence, and Saul saw that he was but a youth, he attempted to dissuade him. But David told him how he had slain the lion and the bear with his naked hands. "The Lord who delivered me from them will deliver me out of the hand of this Philistine," he said.

Then King Saul said: "Go, and the Lord go with thee!"

He had his own armor fetched for David, his helmet of brass, his coat of mail, and his own sword. But David said: "I cannot fight with these. I am not skilled in their use." He put them down, for he knew that each man must win his battles with his own weapons.

Then he took his staff in his hand, his shepherd's bag and sling he hung at his side, and he set out from the camp of Israel. He ran lightly down the hillside, and when he came to the brook which ran at the foot of the hill, he stooped, and choosing five smooth stones from the brook, dropped them into his bag.

The army of King Saul upon one hill, and the host of the Philistines upon the other, looked on in silent wonder. The great giant strode toward David, and when Goliath saw that he was but a youth, ruddy and fair of countenance, his anger knew no bounds.

"Am I a dog, that thou comest to me with sticks?" he shouted. "Do the men of Israel make mock of me to send a child against me? Turn back, or I will give thy flesh to the birds of the air and to the beasts of the field!" Then Goliath cursed David in the name of all his gods.

But no fear came to David's heart. He called out bravely: "Thou comest to me with a sword, and with a spear, and with a shield: but I come to thee in the name of the Lord of hosts, the God of the armies of Israel, whom thou hast defied. This day will the Lord deliver thee into mine hands; and I will smite thee, that all the earth may know that there is a God in Israel!"

Then Goliath rushed forward to meet David, and David ran still more swiftly to meet the giant. He put his hand into his bag and took one of the stones from it. He fitted it into his sling, and his keen eye found the place in the giant's forehead where the helmet joined. He drew his sling, and with all the force of his strong right arm, he hurled the stone.

It whizzed through the air and struck deep into Goliath's forehead. His huge body tottered—then fell crashing to the ground. As he lay with his face upon the earth, David ran swiftly to his side, drew forth the giant's own sword, and severed his huge head from his body.

When the army of Israel saw this, they rose up with a great shout and rushed down the hillside to throw themselves upon the frightened Philistines who were fleeing in terror. When they saw their greatest warrior slain by this lad, they fled toward their own land, leaving their tents and all their riches to be spoiled by the men of Israel.

When the battle was ended, King Saul caused David to be brought before him, and he said: "Thou shalt go no more to the house of thy father, but thou shalt be as mine own son."

So David stayed in the tents of the king, and at length he was given command over the king's armies. All Israel honored him, and long years after, he was made the king in King Saul's stead.

Dolley Madison Saves the National Pride

DOROTHEA PAYNE MADISON

In August 1814, a British army marched on Washington, D.C., thinking that by burning the American capital it could bring an end to the War of 1812. Panic reigned in the city as the red-coated columns approached. Many public records, including the Declaration of Independence, had already been stuffed into linen bags and carted off to Virginia, where they were piled up in a vacant house. Now the roads leading out of town began to fill with fleeing American soldiers and statesmen as well as wagons loaded with families and their valuables.

Dolley Madison, wife of the fourth president, calmly directed evacuation details at the White House. A large portrait of George Washington by Gilbert Stuart hung in the dining room. It would be an unbearable disgrace if it fell into British hands. Mrs. Madison ordered the doorkeeper and gardener to bring it along, but the huge frame was screwed so tightly to the wall that no one could get it down. Minutes ticked by as they tugged and pulled. At last someone found an

*ax. They chopped the frame apart, removed the canvas, and sent it off
for safekeeping. Soon afterward the British entered the District of
Columbia, setting fire to the Capitol and the White House.*

*The rescue of Washington's portrait quickly took its place as one
of Americans' most cherished acts of heroism. This letter, written by
Dolley to her sister, Anna, even as the city fell, speaks to us of unflinch-
ing courage and levelheadedness amid chaos and retreat.*

Tuesday, August 23, 1814

Dear Sister:

My husband left me yesterday morning to join General Winder.
He inquired anxiously whether I had courage or firmness to
remain in the President's house until his return on the morrow,
or succeeding day, and on my assurance that I had no fear but
for him, and the success of our army, he left, beseeching me to
take care of myself, and of the Cabinet papers, public and private. I have since received two dispatches from him, written
with a pencil. The last is alarming, because he desires I should
be ready at a moment's warning to enter my carriage and leave
the city; that the enemy seemed stronger than had at first been
reported, and it might happen that they would reach the city
with the intention of destroying it. I am accordingly ready; I
have pressed as many Cabinet papers into trunks as to fill one
carriage; our private property must be sacrificed, as it is impossible to procure wagons for its transportation.

I am determined not to go myself until I see Mr. Madison safe, so that he can accompany me, as I hear of much hostility toward him. Disaffection stalks around us. My friends and acquaintances are all gone, even Colonel C. with his hundred, who were stationed as a guard in this enclosure. French John, a faithful servant, with his usual activity and resolution, offers to spike the cannon at the gate, and lay a train of powder, which would blow up the British, should they enter the house. To this last proposition I positively object, without being able to make him understand why all advantages in war may not be taken.

Wednesday morning, twelve o'clock. Since sunrise I have been turning my spy-glass in every direction, and watching with unwearied anxiety, hoping to discover the approach of my dear husband and his friends; but, alas! I can descry only groups of military, wandering in all directions, as if there was a lack of arms, or of spirit to fight for their own fireside.

Three o'clock. Will you believe it, my sister? We have had a battle, or skirmish, near Bladensburg, and here I am still, within sound of the cannon! Mr. Madison comes not. May God protect us! Two messengers, covered with dust, come to bid me fly; but here I mean to wait for him. . . . At this late hour a wagon has been procured, and I have had it filled with plate and the most valuable portable articles, belonging to the house. Whether it will reach its destination, the "Bank of Maryland," or fall into the hands of British soldiery, events must determine. Our kind friend, Mr. Carroll, has come to hasten my departure, and in a very bad humor with me, because I insist on waiting until the large picture of General Washington is secured, and it requires to be unscrewed from the wall. This process was found too tedious for these perilous moments; I have ordered the frame to be broken, and the canvas taken out. It is done! And the precious portrait placed in the hands of two gentlemen of New York, for safekeeping. And now, dear sister, I must leave this house, or the retreating army will make me a prisoner of it by filling up the road I am directed to take. When I shall again write to you, or where I shall be tomorrow, I cannot tell!

Dolley

Doors of Daring

HENRY VAN DYKE

Barriers are invitations to courage.

The mountains that inclose the vale
  With walls of granite, steep and high,
Invite the fearless foot to scale
  Their stairway toward the sky.

The restless, deep, dividing sea
  That flows and foams from shore to shore,
Calls to its sunburned chivalry,
  "Push out, set sail, explore!"

The bars of life at which we fret,
  That seem to prison and control,
Are but the doors of daring, set
  Ajar before the soul.

Say not, "Too poor," but freely give;
  Sigh not, "Too weak," but boldly try;
You never can begin to live
  Until you dare to die.

Duty, Honor, Country

Douglas MacArthur

These words come from a speech General Douglas MacArthur delivered at West Point on May 12, 1962. Every cadet entering the United States Military Academy receives a copy of the address. They are great words not only for every soldier, but for every citizen.

Duty. Honor. Country. Those three hallowed words reverently dictate what you ought to be, what you can be, what you will be. They are your rallying points, to build courage when courage seems to fail, to regain faith when there seems to be little cause for faith, to create hope when hope becomes forlorn. . . .

The unbelievers will say they are but words, but a slogan, but a flamboyant phrase. Every pedant, every demagogue, every cynic, every hypocrite, every troublemaker, and, I am sorry to say, some others of an entirely different character, will try to downgrade them even to the extent of mockery and ridicule, but these are some of the things they do. They build your basic character. They mold you for your future roles as the custodians of the nation's defense. They make you strong enough to know when you are weak, and brave enough to face yourself when you are afraid.

They teach you to be proud and unbending in honest failure, but humble and gentle in success; not to substitute words for actions, not to seek the path of comfort, but to face the stress and spur of difficulty and challenge; to learn to stand up in the storm, but to have compassion on those who fail; to master yourself before you seek to master others; to have a heart that is clean, a goal that is high; to learn to laugh yet never forget how to weep; to reach into the future, yet never neglect the past; to be serious, yet never to take yourself too seriously; to be modest so that you will remember the simplicity of true greatness, the open mind of true wisdom, the meekness of true strength.

They give you a temper of the will, a quality of the imagination, a vigor of the emotions, a freshness of the deep springs of life, a temperamental predominance of courage over timidity, of an appetite for adventure over love of ease.

They create in your heart the sense of wonder, the unfailing hope of what next, and the joy and inspiration of life. They teach you in this way to be an officer and a gentleman.

The End of the Scott Expedition

Robert Falcon Scott

In 1910, Captain Robert Falcon Scott, of the British Navy, set sail on a second attempt to reach the South Pole. Two years later, on January 18, 1912, after a treacherous journey across vast stretches of ice-covered Antarctica, Scott and four companions reached their destination, only to find that a rival expedition led by Norwegian explorer Roald Amundsen had beaten them by thirty-five days. They found Amundsen's tent still uncovered by snow.

Disheartened and exhausted, Scott and his party began their seven-hundred-mile homeward trek, a journey that would end in tragedy. Food and fuel ran low, temperatures plummeted, and frostbite worsened daily. On March 3, Scott wrote in his diary: "God help us, we can't keep up this pulling, that is certain. Amongst ourselves we are unendingly cheerful, but what each man feels in his heart I can only guess." On March 16, he wrote: ". . . assuredly the end is not far." And finally, on March 29: "It seems a pity, but I do not think I can write more. R. Scott. . . . For God's sake, look after our people."

Scott and two companions made it to within fifteen miles of a supply camp. Months later, a search party found the bodies in their sleeping bags, half buried in snow. Among the records of the trip, they found this last message by Scott to the public, a farewell letter showing, as Scott wrote in an accompanying note, that "Englishmen can still die with a bold spirit, fighting it out to the end."

T he causes of the disaster are due not to faulty organization but to the misfortune in all risks which had to be undertaken.

1. The loss of pony transport in March 1911 obliged me to start later than I had intended, and obliged the limits of stuff transported to be narrowed.

2. The weather throughout the outward journey, and especially the long gale in 83dg S., stopped us.

3. The soft snow in lower reaches of glacier again reduced pace.

We fought these untoward events with a will and conquered, but it cut into our provision reserve.

Every detail of our food supplies, clothing and depots made on the interior ice-sheet and over that long stretch of 700 miles to the Pole and back, worked out to perfection. The advance party would have returned to the glacier in fine form and with surplus of food, but for the astonishing failure of the man whom we had least expected to fail. Edgar Evans was thought the strongest man of the party.

The Beardmore Glacier is not difficult in fine weather, but on our return we did not get a single completely fine day; this with a sick companion enormously increased our anxieties.

As I have said elsewhere we got into frightfully rough ice and Edgar Evans received a concussion of the brain—he died a natural death, but left us a shaken party with the season unduly advanced.

But all the facts above enumerated were as nothing to the surprise which awaited us on the Barrier. I maintain that our arrangements for returning were quite adequate, and that no one in the world would have expected the temperatures and surfaces which we encountered at this time of the year. On the summit in lat. 85dg, 86dg we had ms20dg, ms30dg. On the Barrier in lat. 80dg, 10,000 feet lower, we had ms30dg in the day, ms47dg at night pretty regularly, with continuous head wind during our day marches. It is clear that these circumstances come on very suddenly, and our wreck is certainly due to this sudden advent of severe weather, which does not seem to have any satisfactory cause. I do not think human beings ever came through such a month as we have come through, and we should have got through in spite of the weather but for the sickening of a second companion, Captain Oates, and a shortage of fuel in our depots for which I cannot account, and finally, but for the storm which has fallen on us within 11 miles of the depot at which we hoped to secure our final supplies.

Surely misfortune could scarcely have exceeded this last blow. We arrived within 11 miles of our old One Ton Camp with fuel for one last meal and food for two days.

For four days we have been unable to leave the tent—the gale howling about us. We are weak, writing is difficult, but for my own sake I do not regret this journey, which has shown that Englishmen can endure hardships, help one another, and meet death with as great a fortitude as ever in the past. We took risks, we knew we took them; things have come out against us, and therefore we have no cause for complaint, but bow to the will of Providence, determined still to do our best to the last. But if we have been willing to give our lives to this enterprise, which is for the honour of our country, I appeal to our countrymen to see that those who depend upon us are properly cared for.

Had we lived, I should have had a tale to tell of the hardihood, endurance, and courage of my companions, which would have stirred the heart of every Englishman. These rough notes and our dead bodies must tell the tale, but surely, surely, a great rich country like ours will see that those who are dependent on us are properly provided for.

R. Scott

For the Love of a Man

JACK LONDON

Friends pull each other through hard times. They bet on each other. They do both—literally—in this excerpt from one of the most popular American adventure stories, The Call of the Wild. *The book tells the story of a dog named Buck, who is adopted by John Thornton, an Alaskan who is the first human being to show him kindness.*

For the most part, Buck's love was expressed in adoration. While he went wild with happiness when Thornton touched him or spoke to him, he did not seek these tokens. Buck was content to adore at a distance. He would lie by the hour, eager, alert, at Thornton's feet, looking up into his face, dwelling upon it, studying it, following with keenest interest each fleeting expression, every movement or change of feature. Or, as chance might have it, he would lie farther away, to the side or rear, watching the outlines of the man and the occasional movements of his body. And often, such was the communion in which they lived, the strength of Buck's gaze would draw John Thornton's head around, and he would return the gaze, without speech, his heart shining out of his eyes as Buck's heart shone out.

But in spite of this great love he bore John Thornton, which seemed to bespeak the soft civilizing influence, the strain of the primitive, which the Northland had aroused in him, remained alive and active. Faithfulness and devotion, things born of fire and roof, were his; yet he retained his wildness and wiliness. He was a thing of the wild, come in from the wild to sit by John Thornton's fire, rather than a dog of the soft Southland stamped with the marks of generations of civilization. Because of his very great love, he could not steal from this man, but from any other man, in any other camp, he did not hesitate an instant; while the cunning with which he stole enabled him to escape detection.

He was older than the days he had seen and the breaths he had drawn. He linked the past with the present, and the eternity behind him throbbed through him in a mighty rhythm to which he swayed as the tides and seasons swayed. He sat by John Thornton's fire, a broad-breasted dog, white-fanged and long-furred; but behind him were the shades of all manner of dogs, half-wolves and wild wolves, urgent and prompting, tasting the savor of the meat he ate, thirsting for the water he drank, scenting the wind with him, listening with him and telling him the sounds made by the wild life in the forest; dictating his moods, directing his actions, lying down to sleep with him when he lay down, and dreaming with him and beyond him and becoming themselves the stuff of his dreams.

So peremptorily did these shades beckon him, that each day mankind and the claims of mankind slipped farther from him. Deep in the forest a call was sounding, and as often as he heard this call, mysteriously thrilling and luring, he felt compelled to turn his back upon the fire and the beaten earth around it, and to plunge into the forest, and on and on, he knew not where or why; nor did he wonder where or why, the call sounding imperiously, deep in the forest. But as often as he gained the soft, unbroken earth and the green shade, the love for John Thornton drew him back to the fire again.

Thornton alone held him. The rest of mankind was as nothing. Chance travelers might praise or pet him; but he was cold under it all, and from a too demonstrative man he would get up and walk away. When Thornton's partners, Hans and Pete, arrived on the long-expected raft, Buck refused to notice them till he learned they were close to Thornton; after that he tolerated them in a passive sort of way, accepting favors from them as though he favored them by accepting. They were of the same large type as Thornton, living close to the earth, thinking simply and seeing clearly; and ere they swung the raft into the big eddy by the sawmill at Dawson, they understood Buck and his ways.

For Thornton, however, his love seemed to grow and grow. He, alone among men, could put a pack upon Buck's back in the summer traveling. Nothing was too great for Buck to do, when Thornton commanded. One day (they had grubstaked themselves from the proceeds of the raft and left Dawson for the headwaters of the Tanana) the men and dogs were sitting on the crest of a cliff which fell away, straight down, to naked bedrock three hundred feet below. John Thornton was sitting near the edge, Buck at his shoulder. A thoughtless whim seized Thornton, and he drew the attention of Hans and Pete to the experiment he had in mind. "Jump, Buck!" he commanded, sweeping his arm out and over the chasm. The next instant he was grappling with Buck on the extreme edge, while Hans and Pete were dragging them back into safety.

"It's uncanny," Pete said, after it was over and they had caught their speech.

Thornton shook his head. "No, it is splendid, and it is terrible, too. Do you know, it sometimes makes me afraid."

"I'm not hankering to be the man that lays hands on you while he's around," Pete announced conclusively, nodding his head toward Buck.

"Py Jingo!" was Hans's contribution. "Not mineself either."

Later on, in the fall of the year, Buck saved John Thornton's life. The three partners were lining a long and narrow poling-boat down a bad stretch of rapids on the Forty Mile Creek. Hans and Pete moved along the bank, snubbing with a thin Manila rope from tree to tree, while Thornton remained in the boat, helping its descent by means of a pole, and shouting directions to the shore. Buck, on the bank, worried and anxious, kept abreast of the boat, his eyes never off his master.

At a particularly bad spot, where a ledge of barely submerged rocks jutted out into the river, Hans cast off the rope, and, while Thornton poled the boat out into the stream, ran down the bank with the end in his hand to snub the boat when it had cleared the ledge. This it did, and was flying downstream in a current as swift as a millrace, when Hans checked it with the rope and checked too suddenly. The boat flirted over and snubbed in to the bank bottom up, while Thornton, flung sheer out of it, was carried downstream toward the worst part of the rapids, a stretch of wild water in which no swimmer could live.

Buck had sprung in on the instant, and at the end of three hundred yards, amid a mad swirl of water, he overhauled Thornton. When he felt him grasp his tail, Buck headed for the bank, swimming with all his splendid strength. But the progress shoreward was slow, the progress downstream amazingly rapid. From below came the fatal roaring where the wild current went wilder and was rent in shreds and spray by the rocks which thrust through like the teeth of an enormous comb. The suck of the water as it took the beginning of the last steep pitch was frightful, and Thornton knew that the shore was impossible. He scraped furiously over a rock, bruised across a second, and struck a third with crushing force. He clutched its slippery top with both hands, releasing Buck, and above the roar of the churning water shouted: "Go, Buck! Go!"

Buck could not hold his own, and swept on downstream, struggling desperately, but unable to win back. When he heard Thornton's command repeated, he partly reared out of the water, throwing his head high, as though for a last look, then turned obediently toward the bank. He swam powerfully and was dragged ashore by Pete and Hans at the very point where swimming ceased to be possible and destruction began.

They knew that the time a man could cling to a slippery rock in the face of that driving current was a matter of minutes, and they ran as fast as they could up the bank to a point far above where Thornton was hanging on. They attached the line with which they had been snubbing the boat to Buck's neck and shoulders, being careful that it should neither strangle him nor impede his swimming, and launched him into the stream. He struck out boldly, but not straight enough into the stream. He discovered the mistake too late, when Thornton was abreast of him and a bare half-dozen strokes away while he was being carried helplessly past.

Hans promptly snubbed with the rope, as though Buck were a boat. The rope thus tightening on him in the sweep of the current, he was jerked under the surface, and under the surface he remained till his body struck against the bank and he was hauled out. He was half-drowned, and Hans and Pete threw themselves upon him, pounding the breath into him and the water out of him. He staggered to his feet and fell down. The faint sound of Thornton's voice came to them, and though they could not make out the words of it, they knew that he was in his extremity. His master's voice acted on Buck like an electric shock. He sprang to his feet and ran up the bank ahead of the men to the point of his previous departure.

Again the rope was attached and he was launched, and again he struck out, but this time straight into the stream. He had miscalculated once, but he would not be guilty of it a second time. Hans paid out the rope, permitting no slack, while Pete kept it clear of coils. Buck held on till he was on a line straight above

Thornton; then he turned, and with the speed of an express train headed down upon him. Thornton saw him coming, and, as Buck struck him like a battering ram, with the whole force of the current behind him, he reached up and closed with both arms around the shaggy neck. Hans snubbed the rope around the tree, and Buck and Thornton were jerked under the water. Strangling, suffocating, sometimes one uppermost and sometimes the other, dragging over the jagged bottom, smashing against rocks and snags, they veered in to the bank.

Thornton came to, belly downward and being violently propelled back and forth across a drift log by Hans and Pete. His first glance was for Buck. Thornton went carefully over Buck's body, when he had been brought around, finding three broken ribs.

"That settles it," he announced. "We camp right here." And camp they did, till Buck's ribs knitted and he was able to travel.

That winter, at Dawson, Buck performed another exploit, not so heroic, perhaps, but one that puts his name many notches higher on the totem pole of Alaskan fame. This exploit was particularly gratifying to the three men; for they stood in need of the outfit which it furnished, and were enabled to make a long-desired trip into the virgin East, where miners had not yet appeared. It was brought about by a conversation in the Eldorado Saloon, in which men waxed boastful of their favorite dogs. Buck, because of his record, was the target for these men, and Thornton was driven stoutly to defend him. At the end of half an hour one man stated that his dog could start a sled with five hundred pounds and walk off with it; a second bragged six hundred for his dog; and a third, seven hundred.

"Pooh! Pooh!" said John Thornton. "Buck can start a thousand pounds."

"And break it out, and walk off with it for a hundred yards?" demanded Matthewson, a Bonanza king, he of the seven hundred vaunt.

"And break it out, and walk off with it for a hundred yards," John Thornton said coolly.

"Well," Matthewson said, slowly and deliberately, so that all could hear, "I've got a thousand dollars that says he can't. And there it is." So saying, he slammed a sack of gold dust of the size of a bologna sausage down upon the bar.

Nobody spoke. Thornton's bluff, if bluff it was, had been called. He could feel a flush of warm blood creeping up his face. His tongue had tricked him. He did not know whether Buck could start a thousand pounds. Half a ton! The enormousness of it appalled him. He had great faith in Buck's strength and had often thought him capable of starting such a load; but never, as now, had he faced the possibility of it, the eyes of a dozen men fixed upon him, silent and waiting. Further, he had no thousand dollars; nor had Hans or Pete.

"I've got a sled standing outside now, with twenty fifty-pound sacks of flour on it," Matthewson went on with brutal directness, "so don't let that hinder you."

Thornton did not reply. He did not know what to say. He glanced from face to face in the absent way of a man who has lost the power of thought and is seeking somewhere to find the thing that will start it going again. The face of Jim O'Brien, a Mastodon king and old-time comrade, caught his eyes. It was as a cue to him, seeming to rouse him to do what he would never have dreamed of doing.

"Can you lend me a thousand?" he asked, almost in a whisper.

"Sure," answered O'Brien, thumping down a plethoric sack by the side of Matthewson's. "Though it's little faith I'm having, John, that the beast can do the trick."

The Eldorado emptied its occupants into the street to see the test. The tables were deserted, and the dealers and gamekeepers came forth to see the outcome of the wager and to lay odds. Several hundred men, furred and mittened, banked around the sled within easy distance. Matthewson's sled, loaded with a thousand pounds of flour, had been standing for a couple of hours, and in the intense cold (it was sixty below zero) the runners had frozen fast to the hard-packed snow. Men offered odds of two to one that Buck could not budge the sled. A quibble arose concerning the phrase "break out." O'Brien contended it was Thornton's privilege to knock the runners loose, leaving Buck to "break it out" from a dead standstill. Matthewson insisted that the phrase included breaking the runners from the frozen grip of the snow. A majority of the men who had witnessed the making of the bet decided in his favor, whereat the odds went up to three to one against Buck.

There were no takers. Not a man believed him capable of the feat. Thornton had been hurried into the wager, heavy with doubt; and now that he looked at the sled itself, the concrete fact, with the regular team of ten dogs curled up in the snow before it, the more impossible the task appeared. Matthewson waxed jubilant.

"Three to one!" he proclaimed. "I'll lay you another thousand at that figure, Thornton. What d'ye say?"

Thornton's doubt was strong in his face, but his fighting spirit was aroused—the fighting spirit that soars above odds, fails to recognize the impossible, and is deaf to all save the clamor for battle. He called Hans and Pete to him. Their sacks were slim, and with his own the three partners could rake together only two hundred dollars. In the ebb of their fortunes, this sum was their total capital; yet they laid it unhesitatingly against Matthewson's six hundred.

The team of ten dogs was unhitched, and Buck, with his own harness, was put into the sled. He had caught the contagion of the excitement, and he felt that in some way he must do a great thing for John Thornton. Murmurs of admiration at his splendid appearance went up. He was in perfect condition, without an ounce of superfluous flesh, and the one hundred and fifty pounds that he weighed were so many pounds of grit and virility. His furry coat shone with the sheen of silk. Down the neck and across the shoulders, his mane, in repose as it was, half bristled and seemed to lift with every movement, as though excess of vigor made each particular hair alive and active. The great breast and heavy forelegs were no more than in proportion with the rest of the body, where the muscles showed in tight rolls underneath the skin. Men felt these muscles and proclaimed them hard as iron, and the odds went down to two to one.

"Gad, sir! Gad, sir!" stuttered a member of the latest dynasty, a king of the Skookum Benches. "I offer you eight hundred for him, sir, before the test, sir, eight hundred just as he stands."

Thornton shook his head and stepped over to Buck's side.

"You must stand off from him," Matthewson protested. "Free play and plenty of room."

The crowd fell silent; only could be heard the voices of the gamblers vainly offering two to one. Everybody acknowledged Buck a magnificent animal, but twenty fifty-pound sacks of flour bulked too large in their eyes for them to loosen their pouch-strings.

Thornton knelt down by Buck's side. He took his head in his two hands and rested cheek on cheek. He did not playfully shake him, as was his wont, or murmur soft love curses, but he whispered in his ear. "As you love me, Buck. As you love me," was what he whispered. Buck whined with suppressed eagerness.

The crowd was watching curiously. The affair was growing mysterious. It seemed like a conjuration. As Thornton got to his feet, Buck seized his mittened hand between his jaws, pressing in with his teeth and releasing slowly, half reluctantly. It was the answer, in terms not of speech but of love. Thornton stepped well back.

"Now, Buck," he said.

Buck tightened the traces, then slacked them for a matter of several inches. It was the way he had learned.

"Gee!" Thornton's voice rang out, sharp in the tense silence.

Buck swung to the right, ending the movement in a plunge that took up the slack and with a sudden jerk arrested his one hundred and fifty pounds. The load quivered and from under the runners arose a crisp crackling.

"Haw!" Thornton commanded.

Buck duplicated the maneuver, this time to the left. The crackling turned into a snapping, the sled pivoting and the runners slipping and grating several inches to the side. The sled was broken out. Men were holding their breaths, intensely unconscious of the fact.

"Now, MUSH!"

Thornton's command cracked out like a pistol-shot. Buck threw himself forward, tightening the traces with a jarring lunge. His whole body was gathered compactly together in the tremendous effort, the muscles writhing and knotting like live things under the silky fur. His great chest was low to the ground, his head forward and down, while his feet were flying like mad, the claws scarring the hard-packed snow in parallel grooves. The sled swayed and trembled, half-started forward. One of his feet slipped, and one man groaned aloud. Then the sled lurched ahead in what appeared a rapid succession of jerks, though it never really came to a dead stop again . . . half an inch . . . an inch . . . two inches. . . . The jerks perceptibly diminished; as the sled gained momentum, he caught them up, till it was moving steadily along.

Men gasped and began to breathe again, unaware that for a moment they had ceased to breathe. Thornton was running behind, encouraging Buck with short, cheery words. The distance had been measured off, and as he neared the pile of firewood which marked the end of the hundred yards, a cheer began to grow and grow, which burst into a roar as he passed the firewood and halted at command. Every man was tearing himself loose, even Matthewson. Hats and mittens were flying in the air. Men were shaking hands, it did not matter with whom, and bubbling over in a general incoherent babel.

But Thornton fell on his knees beside Buck. Head was against head, and he was shaking him back and forth. Those who hurried up heard him cursing Buck, and he cursed him long and fervently, and softly and lovingly.

"Gad, sir! Gad, sir!" spluttered the Skookum Bench king. "I'll give you a thousand for him, sir, a thousand, sir—twelve hundred, sir."

Thornton rose to his feet. His eyes were wet. The tears were streaming frankly down his cheeks. "Sir," he said to the Skookum Bench king, "no, sir. You can go to hell, sir. It's the best I can do for you, sir."

Buck seized Thornton's hand in his teeth. Thornton shook him back and forth. As though animated by a common impulse, the onlookers drew back to a respectful distance, nor were they again indiscreet enough to interrupt.

God Will Provide

Mexican Folktale

This folktale is an adaptation of Aesop's "Hercules and the Wagoner." It teaches the age-old moral that God helps those who help themselves. Good, hard work is often the best way out of a tough spot.

One sunrise two neighboring farmers set out for market in town. Their wagons were piled high with tomatoes that would ripen quickly in the hot noonday sun, so they pushed their horses steadily all morning, not wanting their precious cargoes to spoil on the way.

But the poor beasts were tired by the time they reached the steepest hill outside town, and strain as they might, they could not get up the slope. The wagons sat at the bottom of the hill, with the climbing sun beating down mercilessly.

"There's nothing to do but let them rest," said the first farmer, shrugging. "And come to think of it, I could use a little siesta myself. We've been on the road since sunup. I think I'll lie under this tree for a while."

"But you can't!" his companion exclaimed. "By the time you wake up, your load will be ruined."

"Don't worry, my friend. God will provide. He always does. I'll just say a few prayers before I doze off." He rolled over on his side with a yawn.

The second farmer, meanwhile, strode to the back of his wagon and, putting his shoulder to the rear, began to shove as hard as he could. He yelled at his horse to pull forward, but to no avail. He pushed till the veins stood out on his neck, and he cursed at the top of his lungs, but his cart ascended the hill not one inch.

Just then the Lord and Saint Peter passed along the road as they sometimes did, for often they walk abroad in order to look into men's hearts. The Lord saw the frantic, swearing farmer struggling with his load. He smiled and laid a kind hand on the wheel, and at once the cart rose to the top of the hill.

The Lord passed on with Saint Peter at his side. The Gatekeeper's gaze bent downward, as if he were pondering their every step.

"I don't understand," he said at last. "Why did you help that man? Even as we came upon him, we heard him cursing most irreverently. And yet you did not help his friend, who offered his prayers for your help."

The Lord smiled.

"The man I helped cursed, it's true, but not with his heart. That is just the way he talks to his horse. In his heart, he was thinking fondly of his wife and children and aged parents, who depend on his labor and need him to return with some profit for his toil. He would have stayed there pushing all day. His friend, on the other hand, calls on me only when he believes he needs me. What he thinks of is sleep. So let him have his nap."

The Gorgon's Head

ADAPTED FROM A RETELLING
BY JAMES BALDWIN

Here is a great Greek hero who perseveres to overcome a series of obstacles, any one of which would deter a feeble heart.

L ong ago on a distant island kingdom lived a beautiful woman named Danaeau and her son, a brave and tall youth named Perseus. The king of this island was a man called Polydectes, and he was so pleased by Danaeau's beauty that he wanted her to become his wife. But he was an evil, cruel man, and she did not like him at all, so she refused all of his offers. Polydectes thought Perseus was to blame for this and that if he could find some excuse to send the young man on a far journey, he might force Danaeau to have him whether she wished or not.

To this end he gave a great feast, and announced that every guest was expected to bring a rich present. For he knew that Perseus, being poor, could not afford such a gift.

When the great banquet began, Perseus stood at the door, sorrowfully watching all the wealthy nobles go in, and his face grew red as they pointed at him and sneered, "What has Perseus to give?"

At last the lad grew mad with shame and, hardly knowing what he said, cried out, "See if I do not bring a better present than all of yours together!"

"Hear the boaster!" laughed Polydectes. "And what are you to bring—the head of Medusa?"

"Yes! I will bring that," swore Perseus, and he went away in anger while everyone laughed at him because of his foolish words.

And what was this Medusa's head which he had so rashly promised to bring?

Far, far away, on the very edge of the world, there lived three strange monsters, sisters, called the Gorgons. They had the bodies and faces of women, but they had wings of gold, and terrible claws of brass, and live serpents growing out of their heads instead of hair. They were so awful to look upon that no one could bear the sight of them. Whoever saw their faces was turned to stone. Two of these monsters had charmed lives, and no weapon could ever do them harm. But the youngest, whose name was Medusa, might be killed if indeed anybody could deliver the fatal stroke.

Perseus strode away from the king's palace, feeling sorry that he had ever spoken so rashly. He did not even know how to find the awful Gorgons. He went down to the shore and stood looking out over the sea while the sun went down and the moon rose. Then, all at once, two persons stood before him. Both were tall and noble. They were Hermes, the messenger of the gods, and Athena, the goddess of wisdom. They told Perseus they would help him.

"You must go first to the three Gray Sisters, who live beyond the frozen sea, in the far, far north," said Athena. "They have a secret which nobody knows, and you must force them to tell you. Ask them where you shall find the three Maidens who guard the golden apples of the West. When they have told you, go straight there. The Maidens will give you three things you will need to obtain the terrible head, and they will tell you how to find the home of the Gorgons."

"But I have no ship. How shall I go?" asked Perseus.

"You shall take my winged sandals," said Hermes. He took off the wonderful shoes, and put them on the youth's feet; and before Perseus could thank them for their kindness, he found himself speeding into the sky, swifter than any eagle.

The winged sandals bore him over the sea, straight toward the north. On and on he went, and soon the sea was passed. He flew over cities and towns and a range of snowy mountains covered with mighty forests, and then a vast plain where many rivers wandered, seeking the sea. Then came frozen marshes and a wilderness of snow, and finally an ocean of ice. On and on he winged his way, among toppling icebergs and over frozen billows and through air the sun never warmed, and at last he came to the cavern where the three Gray Sisters dwelled.

These creatures were so old they had forgotten their own age. The long hair that covered their heads had been gray since they were born. They had among them only a single eye and a single tooth, which they passed back and forth from one to another. Perseus heard them mumbling and crooning in their dreary home, and he stood very still and listened.

"We know a secret we will never tell, don't we, sisters?" said one.

"Ha! ha! That we do! That we do!" chattered the others.

"Give me the tooth, sister, that I may feel young and handsome again," said one.

"And give me the eye that I may look out and see the world," said another.

"Ah, yes, yes, yes," mumbled the third, as she took both the tooth and the eye and held them out blindly toward the others.

Quick as thought, Perseus leaped forward and snatched both of the precious things from her hand.

"Where is the tooth? Where is the eye?" screamed the two, reaching out their long arms and groping here and there. "Have you dropped them, sister? Have you lost them?"

"I have your tooth and your eye," said Perseus, "and you shall not touch them again until you tell me your secret. Where are the Maidens who keep the golden apples of the Western Land?"

Then the Gray Sisters wept and coaxed and threatened. They moaned and mumbled and shrieked, but their words did not move him.

"Sisters, we must tell him," at last one said.

"Ah, yes, we must part with the secret to save our eye," said the others.

Then they told him what road he should follow to find the

Maidens; and when they had made everything plain to Perseus, he gave them back their eye and tooth.

"Ha! ha!" they laughed. "Now the golden days of youth have come again!" Perseus leaped into the air again. And from that day to this, though the winds still whistle through their cheerless cave, and the cold waves murmur on the shore of the wintry sea, and the ice mountains topple and crash, no other man has ever seen the three Gray Sisters.

The winged sandals now bore Perseus southward. He left the frozen wilderness behind and soon came to a sunny land, where there were green forests and flowery meadows and hills and valleys, and at last a pleasant garden with all kinds of fruits and blossoms. And here he found the three Maidens of the West dancing and singing around a tree of golden apples.

Perseus told them of his quest, and said he had come to ask them to give him three things to help him fight the Gorgons.

The Maidens answered they would give him not three things but four. One of them gave him a sharp sword, which she fastened to the belt at his waist. Another gave him a shield, which was brighter than any looking glass. The third gave him a magic pouch, which she hung by a long strap over his shoulder. Finally they all three gave him a magic helmet, the Helmet of Darkness; and when they had put it on his head, there was no creature on earth or in the sky that could see him.

Then they told him where he could find the Gorgons, and what he should do to obtain the terrible head and escape alive. Perseus donned the Helmet of Darkness, and sped away toward the farthest edge of the earth. And the three Maidens went back to their tree to sing and to dance and to guard the golden apples until the old world should become young again.

Perseus flew so swiftly it was not long until he had crossed the mighty ocean that encircles the earth and had come to the sunless land that lies beyond. He heard the sound of someone breathing heavily, and he looked around sharply to see where it came from. Among the foul weeds that grew close by the bank of a muddy river there was something glittering in the pale light.

He flew a little nearer, but he did not dare look straight forward, lest he should meet the gaze of a Gorgon, and be changed to stone. Instead, he turned around and held the shining shield before him in such a way that by looking into it he could see objects behind him as in a mirror.

Ah, what a dreadful sight it was! Half hidden among the weeds lay the three monsters, fast asleep, with their golden wings folded about them. Their brazen claws were stretched out as though ready to seize their prey, and their shoulders were covered with sleeping snakes. The two largest of the Gorgons lay with their heads tucked under their wings as birds hide their heads when they go to sleep. But the third, who lay between them, slept with her face turned up to the sky, and Perseus knew she was Medusa.

Very stealthily he went nearer and nearer, always with his back toward the monsters and always looking into his bright shield to see where to go. Then he drew his sharp sword and, dashing it quickly downward, struck a blow so sure, so swift, that the head of Medusa was severed from her shoulders and the black blood gushed like a river from her neck. Quick as thought he thrust the terrible head into his magic pouch, leaped into the air again, and flew away with the speed of wind.

Then the two older Gorgons awoke, and rose with dreadful screams, and spread their great wings to dash after him. They could not see him, for the Helmet of Darkness hid him from their eyes, but they scented the blood of their sister's head, and they followed him, sniffing the air. As he flew he could hear the clatter of their golden wings and the snapping of their horrible jaws. But the winged sandals were swift as the wind, and soon he had left the monsters far behind.

He flew on, toward home, until he passed over a country of sunshine and palm trees and a great river flowing from the south. Here, as he looked down, a strange sight met his eyes: He saw a beautiful girl chained to a rock by the seashore, and far away a huge beast swimming to devour her.

At once Perseus flew down, drew his sharp sword, and cut the chain which held her. By this time the monster was close at hand, lashing the water with its tail and opening its wide jaws so as to swallow both Perseus and the girl. But as it came roaring toward the shore, Perseus lifted the head of Medusa from its pouch and held it high. When the beast saw the dreadful face, it stopped short and was turned into stone. And men say that the stone beast may be seen in that same spot today.

The girl told him her name was Andromeda, and that she was the princess of that land. She had been chained to the rock as an offering to the terrible beast, which was destroying the whole land. At once Perseus asked her to be his wife, and they were married with a great feast, and the two young people lived happily for some time in that sunny place.

But Perseus had not forgotten his mother, so one fine summer day he sailed home, taking Andromeda with him. He left his ship on the beach, and found his mother, and they wept over each other.

Then Perseus went up to the palace of Polydectes with the head of Medusa in his pouch. When he came to the great hall, the evil king sat at his table, with all his nobles on either side, feasting and drinking wine. Perseus stood upon the threshold and called Polydectes by name, but none of the guests knew the stranger, for he was changed by his long journey. He had gone out a boy, and he had come home a man and a great hero.

But Polydectes the Wicked knew him and scornfully called, "Ah, foolish boaster! Have you found it easier to make a promise than to fulfill it?"

"When a promise is made to right a wrong, sometimes the gods help fulfill it," Perseus answered. And turning aside his own eyes, he drew open the pouch, held aloft the Gorgon's head, and cried, "Behold!"

Pale grew Polydectes and his guests as they looked upon the dreadful face. They tried to spring away, but they never rose from their seats. They stiffened, each man where he sat, into a ring of cold gray stones.

Then Perseus turned and left them, went down to his galley by the shore, and sailed away with his mother and his bride.

Henry's Speech at Agincourt

WILLIAM SHAKESPEARE

It would be hard to read Henry's address at Agincourt and escape a brief twinge of regret for not having been one of the "happy few" to fight on St. Crispin's day. The scene (from Shakespeare's King Henry the Fifth*) is the English camp the moment before the battle. The year is 1415. Young King Henry of England has landed a well-equipped army in Normandy and begun a campaign to conquer France. Reaching Agincourt, the English forces found themselves facing a much larger French army. I believe, from my experience, that this speech is the model for all half-time talks given by all football coaches every autumn in America.*

Westmoreland: O that we now had here
   But one ten thousand of those men in England
   That do no work today!

King Henry: What's he that wishes so?
  My cousin Westmoreland? No, my fair cousin.
  If we are mark'd to die, we are enow
  To do our country loss; and if to live,
  The fewer men, the greater share of honour.
  God's will! I pray thee, wish not one man more.
  By Jove, I am not covetous for gold,
  Nor care I who doth feed upon my cost;
  It yearns me not if men my garments wear;
  Such outward things dwell not in my desires;
  But if it be a sin to covet honour,
  I am the most offending soul alive.
  No, faith, my coz, wish not a man from England.
  God's peace! I would not lose so great an honour
  As one man more, methinks, would share from me
  For the best hope I have. O, do not wish one more!
  Rather proclaim it, Westmoreland, through my host,
  That he which hath no stomach to this fight,
  Let him depart; his passport shall be made
  And crowns for convoy put into his purse.
  We would not die in that man's company
  That fears his fellowship to die with us.
  This day is call'd the feast of Crispian.
  He that outlives this day, and comes safe home,
  Will stand a tip-toe when this day is named,
  And rouse him at the name of Crispian.
  He that shall live this day, and see old age,
  Will yearly on the vigil feast his neighbours,

And say, "To-morrow is Saint Crispian."
Then will he strip his sleeve and show his scars,
And say "These wounds I had on Crispin's day."
Old men forget; yet all shall be forgot,
But he'll remember with advantages
What feats he did that day. Then shall our names,
Familiar in his mouth as household words,
Harry the king, Bedford and Exeter,
Warwick and Talbot, Salisbury and Gloucester,
Be in their flowing cups freshly remember'd.
This story shall the good man teach his son;
And Crispin Crispian shall ne'er go by,
From this day to the ending of the world,
But we in it shall be remembered,
We few, we happy few, we band of brothers.
For he to-day that sheds his blood with me
Shall be my brother; be he ne'er so vile,
This day shall gentle his condition;
And gentlemen in England now a-bed
Shall think themselves accursed they were not here,
And hold their manhoods cheap whiles any speaks
That fought with us upon Saint Crispin's day.

If—

Rudyard Kipling

Brave men and women (as well as cowardly men and women) are not born that way; they become that way through their acts. Here are the acts that make us not just grow up, but grow up well.

If you can keep your head when all about you
Are losing theirs and blaming it on you;
If you can trust yourself when all men doubt you,
But make allowance for their doubting too;
If you can wait and not be tired by waiting,
Or, being lied about, don't deal in lies,
Or, being hated, don't give way to hating,
And yet don't look too good, nor talk too wise;

If you can dream—and not make dreams your master;
If you can think—and not make thoughts your aim;
If you can meet with triumph and disaster

And treat those two impostors just the same;
If you can bear to hear the truth you've spoken
Twisted by knaves to make a trap for fools,
Or watch the things you gave your life to broken,
And stoop and build 'em up with worn-out tools;
If you can make one heap of all your winnings

And risk it on one turn of pitch-and-toss,
And lose, and start again at your beginnings
And never breathe a word about your loss;
If you can force your heart and nerve and sinew
To serve your turn long after they are gone,
And so hold on when there is nothing in you
Except the Will which says to them: "Hold on!"

If you can talk with crowds and keep your virtue,
Or walk with kings—nor lose the common touch;
If neither foes nor loving friends can hurt you;
If all men count with you, but none too much;
If you can fill the unforgiving minute
With sixty seconds' worth of distance run—
Yours is the Earth and everything that's in it,
And—which is more—you'll be a Man, my son!

Jack and the Beanstalk

ADAPTED FROM ANDREW LANG

After David, Jack is probably our most famous and beloved giant-slayer. He begins his adventure as a thoughtless boy, but redeems himself through a bravery that rises from a sense of duty to his mother. Courage leads upward, and sooner or later we must all climb our own beanstalks.

O nce upon a time there was a poor widow who lived in a little cottage with her only son, Jack. Jack was a silly, thoughtless boy, but very kind-hearted.

One morning the old woman told her son to go to the market and sell their cow. So Jack started out, but on the way he met a butcher with some beautiful beans in his hand. The butcher told the boy they were of great value and persuaded the silly lad to swap the cow for the beans.

Well, of course, when Jack came home with nothing but a handful of beans to show for their cow, his mother shed many a tear. At that Jack realized his foolishness and felt terrible. "At least," he thought, "I may as well sow the beans." So he planted them in the garden and went sadly to bed.

The next day he got up at daybreak and went into the garden. To his amazement he found that the beans had grown up in the night, and their stalks climbed up and up like a ladder disappearing into the clouds!

"It would be easy to climb it," Jack thought.

So he began to climb, and went up and up the stalk until he had left everything behind—cottage, village, even the church tower. At last he reached the top and found himself in a beautiful country, finely wooded, with lush meadows covered with sheep. A crystal stream ran through the pastures, and nearby stood a fine, strong castle. While he was standing looking at it, an ancient lady came walking along.

"If you please, ma'am," said Jack, "is this your house?"

"No," said the old lady. "That is the castle of a wicked giant who keeps wonderful treasures inside. It is said that someday a young lad will come from the valley below to challenge the giant and win the treasures for his poor mother. Perhaps you are the one. But the task is very difficult and full of peril. Have you the courage to undertake it?"

"I fear nothing when I am doing right," said Jack.

"Then," said the old lady, "you are one of those who slay giants. If you can get into the castle, you may find a hen that lays golden eggs, and a harp that talks, as well as two bags full of gold. If you can get them, they will be a great comfort to your poor mother."

So Jack marched forward and knocked at the castle gate. The door was opened in a minute or two by a frightful giantess, with one great eye in the middle of her forehead. At once she grabbed Jack and dragged him inside.

"Ho, ho!" she laughed terribly. "I've been needing somebody to clean the knives, and shine the boots, and make the fires. You will be my servant. But I must hide you whenever the giant is home, for he has eaten up all my other servants, and you would be a dainty morsel, too, my lad."

Well, Jack was very much frightened, as you can imagine, but he struggled to be brave and make the best of things.

"I am quite ready to serve you," he said, "only I beg you to hide me from your husband, for I should not like to be eaten at all."

"That's a good boy," said the giantess. "It is lucky you did not scream when you saw me, or he would have heard you and eaten you for supper, as he has done with so many others. Come here, child. Go into my closet. He never looks in there, and you will be safe."

She opened a huge door that stood in the great hall and shut him in. But the keyhole was so large that it admitted plenty of air, and he could see everything that took place through it. By and by he heard a heavy tramp on the stairs, like the lumbering along of a great cannon, and then a voice like thunder cried out:

> Fe, fi, fo, fum,
> I smell the blood of an Englishman.
> Be he alive or be he dead,
> I'll grind his bones to make my bread.

"Wife," cried the giant, "there is a man in the castle. Let me have him for supper."

"You have grown old and stupid," said the lady in her loud tones. "You smell only the dinner I have cooked for you. There, sit down and have a good supper."

So the giant sat down at his table. Jack watched him through the keyhole and was amazed to see him swallow a whole roast pig in one bite. Then he drank a whole barrel of ale in one gulp.

When the supper was ended he asked his wife to bring him his hen that laid the golden eggs. The giantess went away, and soon returned with a little brown hen, which she placed on the table before her husband.

"Lay!" said the giant, and instantly the hen laid a golden egg.

"Lay!" said the giant, and she laid another.

"Lay!" he repeated, and again a golden egg appeared on the table.

After a while he put the hen down on the floor, and called on his wife to bring him his moneybags. The giantess went and soon returned with two large bags over her shoulders, which she set down by her husband. The giant took out heaps and heaps of golden pieces, and counted them, and put them in piles, till he was tired of the amusement. Then he swept them all back into their bags.

"I think I will take a nap," he said to his wife. "But first, bring me my harp, for I will have a little music."

So the giantess went away and returned with a beautiful harp. The framework sparkled with diamonds and rubies, and the strings were all of gold.

"Play!" said the giant, and the harp played a very soft, sad song.

"Play something merrier!" said the giant, and the harp played a merry tune.

"Now play me a lullaby," roared the giant. The harp played a sweet lullaby, and its master fell asleep.

Jack stole softly out of the closet and peeped into the huge kitchen to make sure the giantess was not looking. Then he crept up to the giant's chair and quietly gathered the bags of money, and the wonderful hen, and finally the magic harp. Then he ran as fast as he could—but just as he got to the door, the harp called out, "Master! Master!"

And the giant woke up!

With a tremendous roar he sprang from his seat, and in two strides he reached the door.

Jack was very nimble and fled like lightning. The giant came on fast and stretched out his great hand to catch the boy. But Jack darted away, and ran for the top of the beanstalk, and climbed down through the clouds as fast as his feet would move.

He gave a great sigh of relief when he reached his own garden, only to look up and behold the giant climbing down after him!

"Mother! Mother!" cried Jack. "Make haste and bring me the ax!"

His mother ran to him with a hatchet, and Jack began to chop away. But the giant was getting closer and closer.

"Mother, stand out of the way!" Jack yelled. With one last blow he cut the tree stem through and jumped back from the spot.

Down came the giant with a terrible crash, and broke his neck, and stretched dead from one end of the garden to the other.

Well, of course, Jack's poor old mother was scared out of her wits, for it wasn't every day that a giant came crashing down in her garden. But Jack told her all about his adventure, and showed her the bags of money, and how the wonderful hen could lay golden eggs, and how the magic harp could play and sing.

Jack's mother was glad to have such treasures. But she was even more grateful to have her son back safe and sound and proud of him for his courage.

"Yesterday I worried that you were only a foolish and thoughtless boy," she said. "But today you've shown how brave you can be. Now I know you are destined to climb the ladder of fortune, just as you climbed the beanstalk."

So together they buried the wicked giant, then went inside to count their blessings.

Jinkyswoitmaya

C. H. CLAUDY

This story is from The Youth's Companion, *a Boston magazine that from 1827 until 1929 provided instructive and entertaining reading for American children. Here's a great tale about putting yourself on the line.*

A proverb has it that "one man's meat is another man's poison," and true enough it is that what one assimilates with pleasure another can only take with pain. The "water" was a terror to Jinks for reasons which will appear anon; but he had resources of courage in other matters, which, for all they called him a coward, proved him a hero after all.

"It was in the spring of 1897," says Mr. C. H. Claudy, writing in *The Youth's Companion,* "while I was employed on botanical and geological work in Alaska, that I made the acquaintance of 'Jinkyswoitmaya,' whom we called 'Jinks' for short. He was

75

the son of a Russian 'claim-jumper' and an Aleut Indian squaw, and he lived in the little village of Nutchek, Hinchinbrook Island, Prince William Sound.

"Jinks had had rather an unhappy life, for he was, in the estimation of his companions, a coward; he had an innate fear of water. Jinks could not be induced to enter a canoe for any purpose whatever, and on that account he was the scorn of the island, for the Aleuts sport and hunt on the sea as if it were their natural element. But Jinks is no physical coward, and this is the story of how I found it out.

"I had been in the village just two days, when we had one of those terrific rainstorms that occasionally visit the Alaskan coast late in the spring. For three days and nights it rained in sheets. During my enforced idleness I made the acquaintance of Jinks, who could speak a little English, and speedily became fond of me, because I never snubbed him nor spoke his name with the obnoxious Aleutian adjective which means 'one who is afraid' at the end of it.

"Jinks was then about fifteen years old, but strong and wiry, and more than ordinarily bright.

"It was on the third day of our acquaintance, I think, that Jinks told me of the wonderful view from a plateau of a mountain on the island. He said it could be reached by about five hours' climbing. This view, I thought, must be remarkable indeed, and so it happened that, when Jinks shyly proffered his services as guide, I made ready to go as soon as the rain should cease.

"After waiting a day for the streams to subside and the wet ground to dry, we started. We carried a knapsack of food, a canteen of cold tea, a rifle, a sheath-knife apiece, forty feet of three-eighths rope, a hatchet, and a binocular.

"Tramping for an hour steadily west, we came to the foot of Mount Kenia, a hill some four thousand feet high, halfway up which was the wondrous view. Then our difficulties began. The way lay through dense woods for awhile, the ground getting steeper and steeper.

"Now and then a stone would start from our feet and go bounding down the mountain, smashing into trees, rebounding, going on again, until finally stopped by a tangle of underbrush; or, escaping that, it would go on and on until only the echoes of its crashing descent told that it was still on its way. The heavy rain had made the ground easy to our feet, but occasionally the foothold would prove treacherous, and we would slip down on our faces. Several times we came to banks so steep and slippery it seemed as if we were stalled; but Jinks could climb like a monkey, and would crawl up ahead somehow, fasten the rope to a tree and let it down to me, that I might haul myself bodily up after him. We finally reached the end of our climb, at a point about twenty-five hundred feet above the sea level.

"Here we turned to the right, on a natural road of rock, traversing a sort of miniature canaton.

"At the end of half an hour's walk we found ourselves at a standstill, brought up against a blank rock wall thirty feet in height. Nothing disconcerted, Jinks tied the rope about his waist, kicked off his disreputable footwear, and began to climb the wall. How he did it I don't know, for I found it difficult even with the help of the rope he let down to me.

"Once arrived on top, I soon forgot all my tribulations in the wonderful sight. We were on a narrow plateau, perhaps fifty feet wide—a rift in the mountain, which rose in sheer rock walls on each side of us at a distance of a quarter of a mile. A thin line of trees was ahead of me, and beyond them the ocean. Going through the trees, I found myself on the edge of a precipice, with the Pacific Ocean spread out before me.

"Directly in front the rock sloped away steeply for about forty feet, then took an abrupt dive downward, going sheer to the sea in a perpendicular line, about three thousand feet.

"The Alaskan gulf below looked like a huge panorama. Away off on the horizon I could see, with the aid of my glass, the white sails of a hull-down ship. On each side of me stretched away in limitless perspective the Alaskan continuation of the Rocky Mountains—snow-capped always. I will not attempt to describe the vast and desolate scene over which brooded such a silence, accentuated by the occasional single sad call of a gull.

"For perhaps the half of an hour we looked and said nothing. Jinks appeared quite satisfied with my first involuntary expression of delight at the picture, and I did not insult his perceptions by attempting to explain to him how fine I thought it.

"Then we lunched, and after that I walked a rod or two along the brink of the incline and sat down on a little knoll of grass-covered earth, letting my feet hang over on the rock slope below, and prepared to enjoy the changing lights and shadows of the clouds on the sunlit sea, while Jinks went to sleep reclining against a tree directly behind me.

"Then it happened! As I was sitting there peacefully, my

thoughts on anything but the recent rainstorm, the little knoll, its cohesive force loosened by the water it contained, gently detached itself from the rock and slid, with me on it, swiftly down the forty feet of rock slope toward the brink beyond.

"As I went down that terrible slide, my first thought was to jump to safety, my next to spread out and attempt to catch on some projection of rock, and my last a prayer for help. Jinks says I screamed and woke him, but I have no recollection of it. In three or four seconds I had arrived at the edge, convinced that another instant would see me hurtling through the air to the rocks three thousand feet below. On the very edge I stopped, caught on a small uprising bit of rock. I was flat on my back, my arms extended on either side of me and above my head. I was bent in the form of a bow; my body from my waist down was over the brink.

"I did not faint and I was not frightened, which sounds absurd, I know; but it is true. Scientists will tell you that in moments of great and sudden danger, the instinct of self-preservation over-comes mere fear. Be that as it may, I was cool, calm, and much alive to my very slim chance of escape. I could not move. I don't mean that I was held, or that I was paralyzed, but I knew that if I should try to move I must fall over the brink.

"My senses were abnormally keen. I heard the cry of a gull so clearly that I thought it very close, but just then the bird came into my range of vision and I saw it was a long distance away. Jinks's shouting from forty feet above seemed right at my ear— by straining my eyes upward I could see the top of his head—but as he was excited and talked Aleutian, I could not understand him. Turning my eyes the other way and looking toward where my feet should have been, I could see a little strip of sea, the horizon, and the sails of a ship. I remembered I had seen a ship before; I tried to think when, but could not. It bothered my sense of location to see only the sails of a ship when it was between me and the horizon, but then I reflected that its hull was in the zone I could not see.

"I did not think of ways to extricate myself, because in one mental flash I knew my only hope was in Jinks and the rope, and I knew he had left it tied to the tree where he had fastened it for me to climb over the rocky wall at the end of the canaton. A little bit of earth, loosened from above in some way, struck me gently in the face. What if a large amount should come down on me before Jinks could get back with the rope?

"'*But it won't—I'm quite sure it won't—Jinks will be here in a minute now—and then—and then—I'll get out of this mess—the rope—*' and then a horrible thought: '*Suppose the rope is not long enough to reach?*'

"Hope is, in a way, the father of fear, and fear came to me now—with the nearness of relief. I was cold. I didn't tremble; I suppose I was too much afraid that if I did I must fall over the brink. But I was very much frightened by my thought that perhaps the rope would not be long enough to reach me.

"Although it seemed to me that I had been hanging a long time on the edge of the precipice, I realized that I thought so simply from the swiftness and number of my impressions. I tried really to calculate the time, and finally decided I had been there nearly twenty minutes; but that estimate was excessive.

"As the fright in a measure subsided, my body ached in protest against the strained position of the muscles; and then suddenly I forgot pain.

"I heard Jinks. 'Comin' now, misser. Got rope, get up minute now—' finishing off with a long string of Aleutian, which, although incomprehensible, was very comforting. I could not see anything of him, except once in a while the top of his head. It occurred to me, however, that there was really nothing to prevent my turning my head on one side. This I did, very slowly and carefully; and at last, by dint of much straining of eyes, I was able to see Jinks away above me, and in a curiously inverted and distorted perspective, working madly to get the rope untangled.

"In a moment he had finished, and then I had the impatient pleasure of seeing the rope coming slowly down the rock face, twisting and turning, like a thin, long snake. It was curious to watch, because it was all seen out of the corner of my eye—seen as one sees in a dream—shapeless, vague, and yet painfully real.

"Now I heard nothing, felt nothing, neither pain nor fright—saw nothing but this travesty of a snake coming slowly towards me. Slowly crawling, sliding, stopping and coming on down, catching on bits of rock and dropping again, it gradually came nearer. Of course it really came down in a few seconds— just as fast as Jinks could pay it out—but impatience and the abnormally acute state of my nerves made it seem a long time. And then it stopped—just six inches above my hand!

"My arms were stretched to their fullest extent, but the rope did not reach my hands. It did not seem to me to matter much; it must have been that I supposed Jinks had not finished paying out all the rope. Then, after a moment, the rope receded some four or five feet, underwent sundry gyrations, and Jinks disappeared from view. Then the rope descended again, this time with about a foot to spare.

"I held my breath, got a good firm grip with one hand, then with the other; and then, putting my weight on it slowly and timorously, afraid it might give in some way, I began to haul myself up. At last I got my feet on the rock, and the rest was easy. Turning on my face, I could help my arms in their task of hauling by sticking my toes into cracks and on projections, as I had seen Jinks do. Halfway up I had a terrible moment; the rope seemed to give a little, and at the same time I heard a smothered cry from Jinks.

"Now I was but ten feet from the top—now eight—now six—four—three feet—another haul and I was almost there— one foot—safety!

"And then I understood why Jinks was not in sight. He lay at full length on his face, his arms locked round the tree he had used as a pillow earlier in the day, the rope knotted around one ankle. The rope had not been long enough, and Jinks had lengthened it with his own body!

"Anyone who has ever attempted to remain suspended by the arms for more than a few seconds will have some faint idea of what poor Jinks must have suffered on that rack. I weigh one hundred and eighty pounds. The pain he endured without a murmur can be indicated by results. One of his arms was out of joint; that accounted for the sudden give in the rope and the smothered cry. The flesh on the ankle where the rope had been tied was cruelly crushed and bruised.

"Except for seeing him lying there suffering that I might live, I must have fainted away in reaction from the nervous strain. What I did do was perhaps as weak, but I trust excusable. I fell on my face beside Jinks, with one arm round his neck, and burst into sobs. In a moment he was sitting up, his dark face shining with joy, in spite of his pain, that he had saved 'misser' from death.

"I bound up his poor, crushed foot, pulled his arm back into place, and with infinite difficulty helped him home. We arrived just before midnight. We were nursed back to health and strength, and so loud were my praises of Jinks, he soon became the hero of the town. Through the aid of the missionary, I was enabled to make them all understand what a really brave fellow he was, and what an heroic thing he had done in risking his life and enduring pain that another might live.

"Jinks carries a wonderful watch now—and inside the cover is the inscription, 'From a grateful man to a brave one.'"

The Leopard's Revenge

AFRICAN FOLKTALE

Courage involves knowing what to fear, but that in itself is not enough, as this African folktale reminds us. The father leopard of this story may be circumspect, but his taking revenge on a weaker, innocent party is hardly courageous.

Once a leopard cub strayed from his home and ventured into the midst of a great herd of elephants. His mother and father had warned him to stay out of the way of the giant beasts, but he did not listen. Suddenly, the elephants began to stampede, and one of them stepped on the cub without even knowing it. Soon afterward, a hyena found his body and went to tell his parents.

"I have terrible news," he said. "I've found your son lying dead in the field."

The mother and father leopard gave great cries of grief and rage.

"How did it happen?" the father demanded. "Tell me who did this to our son! I will never rest until I have my revenge!"

"The elephants did it," answered the hyena.

"The elephants?" asked the father leopard, quite startled. "You say it was the elephants?"

"Yes," said the hyena, "I saw their tracks."

The leopard paced back and forth for a few minutes, growling and shaking his head.

"No, you are wrong," he said at last. "It was not the elephants. It was the goats. The goats have murdered my boy!"

And at once he bounded down the hill and sprang upon a herd of goats grazing in the valley below, and in a violent rage killed as many as he could in revenge.

Liberty or Death

PATRICK HENRY

A member of Virginia's House of Burgesses and the first Virginia Committee of Correspondence, fierce opponent of the Stamp Act, and delegate to the Continental Congress in 1774–1775, Patrick Henry (1736–1799) was one of the colonies' foremost patriots in the growing revolutionary cause. His oratory gave him lasting fame, and today he is remembered mainly for the fiery speech he gave to the Second Virginia Convention on March 23, 1775, at St. John's Church in Richmond. The question before the Convention was whether to arm the Virginia militia to fight the British. Patrick Henry knew the moment had come for the colonies to gather their strength and commit themselves to action.

M r. President, it is natural to man to indulge in the illusions of hope. We are apt to shut our eyes against a painful truth—and listen to the song of that siren, till she transforms us into beasts. Is this the part of wise men, engaged in a great and arduous struggle for liberty? Are we disposed to be of the number of those who, having eyes, see not, and having ears, hear not, the things which so nearly concern their temporal salvation? For my part, whatever anguish of spirit it might cost, I am willing to know the whole truth; to know the worst, and to provide for it. . . .

There is no longer any room for hope. If we wish to be free—if we mean to preserve inviolate those inestimable privileges for which we have been so long contending—if we mean not basely to abandon the noble struggle in which we have been so long engaged, and which we have pledged ourselves never to abandon until the glorious object of our contest shall be obtained—we must fight!—I repeat it, sir, we must fight! An appeal to arms, and to the God of Hosts, is all that is left us!

They tell us, sir, that we are weak—unable to cope with so formidable an adversary. But when shall we be stronger? Will it be the next week, or the next year? Will it be when we are totally disarmed, and when a British guard shall be stationed in every house? Shall we gather strength by irresolution and inaction? Shall we acquire the means of effectual resistance by lying supinely on our backs, and hugging the delusive phantom of Hope, until our enemies shall have bound us hand and foot? Sir, we are not weak, if we make a proper use of those means which the God of nature hath placed in our power. Three millions of people, armed in the holy cause of liberty, and in such a country as that which we possess, are invincible by any force which our enemy can send against us. Besides, sir, we shall not fight our battles alone. There is a just God who presides over the destinies of nations; and who will raise up friends to fight our battles for us. The battle, sir, is not to the strong alone; it is to the vigilant, the active, the brave. Besides, sir, we have no election. If we were base enough to desire it, it is now too late to retire from the contest. There is no retreat, but in submission and slavery! Our chains are forged, their clanking may be heard on the plains of Boston! The war is inevitable—and let it come! I repeat it, sir, let it come!

It is in vain, sir, to extenuate the matter. Gentlemen may cry, peace, peace—but there is no peace. The war is actually begun! The next gale that sweeps from the north will bring to our ears the clash of resounding arms! Our brethren are already in the field! Why stand we here idle? What is it that gentlemen wish? What would they have? Is life so dear, or peace so sweet, as to be purchased at the price of chains and slavery? Forbid it, Almighty God! I know not what course others may take; but as for me, give me liberty, or give me death!

The Life Heroic

TRADITIONAL

I like the man who faces what he must
    With step triumphant and a heart of cheer;
    Who fights the daily battle without fear;
Sees his hopes fail, yet keeps unfaltering trust
That God is God; that somehow, true and just,
    His plans work out for mortals. Not a tear
    Is shed when fortune, which the world holds dear,
Falls from his grasp. Better with love a crust
Than living in dishonor; envies not,
    Nor loses faith in man, but does his best,
Nor ever murmurs at his humbler lot,
    But with a smile and words of hope gives zest
To every toiler. He alone is great
Who by a life heroic conquers fate.

The Minotaur

ADAPTED FROM ANDREW LANG

The Greek myth of the thread leading Theseus through King Minos's labyrinth is a story of compassion guiding courage. There are two heroes here: Theseus, who ventures into the maze to save his fellow Athenians, and Ariadne, who searches her heart and realizes she must defy her own father in order to save the doomed Athenians from a cruel fate. Conscience is the root of real courage.

T his story begins in Athens, one of the greatest and most noble cities of ancient Greece. At the time it takes place, however, Athens was only a little town, perched on the top of a cliff rising out of the plain, two or three miles from the sea. King Aegeus, who ruled Athens in those days, had just welcomed home a son he had not seen since the child's birth, a youth name Theseus, who was destined to become one of Greece's greatest heroes.

Aegeus was overjoyed at having his son home at last, but

Theseus could not help but notice moments when the king seemed distracted and sad. Gradually, Theseus began to sense the same melancholy among the people of Athens. Mothers were silent, fathers shook their heads, and young people watched the sea all day, as if they expected something fearful to come from it. Many of the Athenian youth seemed to be missing, and were said to have gone to visit friends in faraway parts of Greece. At last Theseus decided to ask his father what troubled the land.

"I'm afraid you've come home at an unhappy time," Aegeus sighed. "There is a curse upon Athens, a curse so terrible and strange that not even you, Prince Theseus, can deal with it."

"Tell me all," said Theseus, "for though I am but one man, yet the ever-living gods protect me and help me."

"The trouble is an old one," Aegeus said. "It dates to a time when young men came to Athens from all over Greece and other lands to take part in contests in running, boxing, wrestling, and foot races. The son of the great Minos, king of Crete, was among the contestants, and he died while he was here. His death is still a puzzle to me. Some say it was an accident; others say he was murdered by jealous rivals. At any rate, his comrades fled in the night, bearing the news to Crete.

"The sea was black with King Midas's ships when he arrived seeking vengeance. His army was far too powerful for us. We went humbly out of the city to meet him and ask for mercy. 'This is the mercy I will show you,' he said. 'I will not burn your city, I will not take your treasures, and I will not make your people my captives. But every seven years, you must pay a tribute. You must swear to choose by lot seven youths and seven maidens, and send them to me.' We had no choice but to agree. Every seven years, a ship with black sails arrives from Crete and bears away the captives. This is the seventh year, and the coming of the ship is at hand."

"And what happens to them once they reach Crete?" Theseus asked.

"We do not know, because they never return. But the sailors of Minos say he places them in a strange prison, a kind of maze, called the Labyrinth. It is full of dark winding ways, cut in the solid rock, and therein lives a horrible monster called the Minotaur. This monster has the body of a man, but his head is the head of a bull, and his teeth are the teeth of a lion, and he devours everyone he meets. That, I fear, is the fate of our Athenian youth."

"We could burn the black-sailed ship when it arrives, and slay its sailors," Theseus said.

"Yes, we could," answered Aegeus, "but then Minos would return with his fleet and his army, and destroy all of Athens."

"Then let me go as one of the captives," said Theseus, rising to his feet, "and I will slay the Minotaur. I am your son and heir, and it is only right that I try to free Athens of this awful curse."

Aegeus tried to persuade his son that such a plan was useless, but Theseus was determined, and when the ship with black sails touched the shore, he joined the doomed group. His father came to tell him goodbye for the last time, weeping bitterly.

"If you do manage to come back alive," he said to Theseus, "lower the black sails as you approach, and hoist white sails in their place, so that I may know you did not die in the Labyrinth."

"Do not worry," Theseus told him. "Look for white sails. I will return in triumph." As he spoke, the dark ship put to sea, and soon sailed past the horizon.

After many days' sailing, the ship reached Crete. The Athenian prisoners were marched to the palace, where King Minos sat on his gilded throne, surrounded by his chiefs and princes, all gloriously clothed in silken robes and jewels of gold. Minos, a dark-faced man, with touches of white in his hair and long beard, sat with his elbow on his knee, and his chin in his hand, and he fixed his eyes on the eyes of Theseus. Theseus bowed and then stood erect, with his eyes on the eyes of Minos.

"You are fifteen in number," Minos said at last, "and my law claims only fourteen."

"I came of my own will," answered Theseus.

"Why?" asked Minos.

"The people of Athens have a mind to be free, O King."

"There is a way," said Minos. "Slay the Minotaur, and you are free of my tribute."

"I am minded to slay him," said Theseus, and as he spoke, there was a stir in the throng of chiefs and princes, and a beautiful young woman glided through them, and stood a little behind the throne. This was Ariadne, the daughter of Minos, a wise and tender-hearted maiden. Theseus bowed low, and again stood erect, with his eyes on the face of Ariadne.

"You speak like a king's son," Minos said with a smile. "Perhaps one who has never known hardship."

"I have known hardship, and my name is Theseus, Aegeus's son. I have come to ask you to let me face the Minotaur alone.

If I cannot slay it, my companions will follow me into the Labyrinth."

"I see," Minos said. "Very well. The king's son wishes to die alone. Let him do so."

The Athenians were led upstairs and along galleries, each to a chamber more rich and beautiful than they had seen before in their dreams. Each was taken to a bath, and washed and clothed in new garments, and then treated to a lavish feast. None had the appetite to eat, though, except Theseus, who knew he would need his strength.

That night, as he was preparing for bed, Theseus heard a soft knock at his door, and suddenly Ariadne, the king's daughter, was standing in his room. Once again Theseus gazed into her eyes, and saw there a kind of strength and compassion he had never known before.

"Too many of your countrymen have disappeared into my father's Labyrinth," she said quietly. "I have brought you a dagger, and I can show you and your friends the way to flee."

"I thank you for the dagger," Theseus answered, "but I cannot flee. If you wish to show me a way, show me the way to the Minotaur."

"Even if you are strong enough to kill the monster," Ariadne whispered, "you will need to find your way out of the Labyrinth. It is made of so many dark twists and turns, so many dead ends and false passages, not even my father knows the secrets of its windings. If you are determined to go forward with your plan, you must take this with you." She took from her gown a spool of gold thread, and pressed it into Theseus's hand.

"As soon as you get inside the Labyrinth," she said, "tie the end of the thread to a stone and hold tight to the spool as you wander through the maze. When you are ready to come back, the thread will be your guide."

Theseus gazed at her, hardly knowing what to say. "Why are you doing this?" he finally asked. "If your father finds out, you'll be in great danger."

"Yes," Ariadne answered slowly, "but if I had not acted, you and your friends would be in far greater danger."

And Theseus knew then that he loved her.

The next morning Theseus was led to the Labyrinth. As soon as the guards shut him inside, he fastened one end of the thread to a pointed rock, and began to walk slowly, keeping firm hold of the precious string. He made his way down the broadest corridor, from which others turned off to the right and left, until he came to a wall. He retraced his steps, and tried another hallway, and then another, always stopping every few feet to listen for the monster. He passed through many dark, winding passages, sometimes coming to places he had already been before, but gradually descending further and further into the Labyrinth. Finally he reached a room heaped high with bones, and he knew now he was very near the beast.

He sat still, and from far away he heard a faint sound, like the end of the echo of a roar. He stood up and listened keenly. The sound came nearer and louder, not deep like the roar of a bull, but more shrill and thin. Theseus stooped quickly and scooped up a handful of dirt from the floor of the Labyrinth, and with his other hand drew his dagger.

The roars of the Minotaur came nearer and nearer. Now his feet could be heard thudding along the echoing floor. There was a heavy rustling, then sniffing, then silence. Theseus moved to the shadowy corner of the narrow path and crouched there. His heart was beating quickly. On came the Minotaur—it caught sight of the crouching figure, gave a great roar, and rushed straight for it. Theseus leaped up and, dodging to one side, dashed his handful of dirt into the beast's eyes.

The Minotaur bellowed in pain. It rubbed its eyes with its monstrous hands, shrieking and confused. It tossed its great head up and down, and it turned around and around, feeling with its hands for the wall. It was quite blind. Theseus drew his dagger, crept up behind the monster, and quickly slashed at its legs. Down fell the Minotaur, with a crash and a roar, biting at the rocky floor with its lion's teeth, waving its hands, and clawing at the empty air. Theseus waited for his chance, when the clutching hands rested, and then three times he drove the sharp blade through the heart of the Minotaur. The body leaped, and lay still.

Theseus kneeled and thanked all the gods, and when he had finished his prayer, he took his dagger and hacked off the head of the Minotaur. With the head in his hand, he began following the string out of the Labyrinth. It seemed he would never come out of those dark, gloomy passages. Had the thread snapped somewhere, and had he, after all, lost his way? But still he followed it anxiously, until at last he came to the entrance, and he sank to the ground, worn out with his struggle and his wanderings.

"I don't know what miracle caused you to come out of the Labyrinth alive," Minos said when he saw the monster's head, "but I will keep my word. I promised you freedom if you slew the Minotaur. You and your comrades may go. Now let there be peace between your people and mine. Farewell."

Theseus knew he owed his life and his country's freedom to Ariadne's courage, and he knew he could not leave without her. Some say he asked Minos for her hand in marriage, and that the king gladly consented. Others say she stole onto the departing ship at the last minute without her father's knowledge. Either way, the two lovers were together when the anchor lifted and the dark ship sailed away from Crete.

But this happy ending is mixed with tragedy, as stories sometimes are. For the Cretan captain of the vessel did not know he was to hoist white sails if Theseus came home in triumph, and King Aegeus, as he anxiously watched the waters from a high cliff, spied the black sails coming over the horizon. His heart broke at once, and he fell from the towering cliff into the sea, which is now called the Aegean.

The Mouse Who Was Afraid

RETOLD BY CATHERINE T. BRYCE

Sometimes the size and strength of a body mean less than the kind of heart it carries inside. All the muscle in the world can't make up for the heart that's not brave.

Once there was a little gray mouse. He lived in the same house as an old gray cat. The little mouse was afraid of the cat.

"How happy I would be but for that old cat," he said. "I am afraid of her all the time. I wish I were a cat."

A fairy heard the little mouse say this. She felt sorry for him. So she turned him into a big gray cat.

At first he was very happy. But one day a dog ran after him.

"Oh, dear!" he said. "It is not much fun to be a cat. I am afraid of that dog all the time. I wish I were a big dog."

Again the fairy heard him. She felt sorry for the old gray cat. So she turned him into a big dog.

Once more he felt happy. Then one day he heard a lion roar.

"Oh, just hear that lion!" he cried. "I am afraid when I hear him. It is not so safe to be a dog after all. How I wish I were a lion. Then I would be afraid of no one."

Off he ran to the fairy.

"Dear fairy," he said, "please turn me into a big, strong lion."

Again the fairy was sorry for him. She made him into a big, strong lion.

One day a man tried to kill the lion. Once more he ran to the fairy.

"What now?" asked the fairy.

"Make me into a man, dear fairy," he cried. "Then no one can make me afraid."

"Make you into a man!" cried the fairy. "No, indeed, I will not. A man must have a brave heart. You have only the heart of a mouse. So a mouse you shall become again, and a mouse you shall stay."

So saying, she turned him back into a little gray mouse, and away he ran to his old home.

The Mutiny

ALPHONSE DE LAMARTINE

This crossing will stand forever as a triumph of unyielding courage and perseverance over fear of the unknown. It's a great episode to remember whenever we encounter rough passages in our own lives. The year, of course, is 1492.

When Columbus left the Canaries to pass with his three small ships into the unknown seas, the eruptions of Teneriffe illuminated the heavens and were reflected in the sea. This cast terror into the minds of his seamen. They thought that it was the flaming sword of the angel who expelled the first man from Eden, and who now was trying to drive back in anger those presumptuous ones who were seeking entrance to the forbidden and unknown seas and lands. But the admiral passed from ship to ship explaining to his men, in a simple way, the action of volcanoes, so that the sailors were no longer afraid.

But as the peak of Teneriffe sank below the horizon, a great sadness fell upon the men. It was their last beacon, the farthest sea-mark of the Old World. They were seized with a nameless terror and loneliness.

Then the admiral called them around him in his own ship, and told them many stories of the things they might hope to find in the wonderful new world to which they were going—of the lands, the islands, the seas, the kingdoms, the riches, the vegetation, the sunshine, the mines of gold, the sands covered with pearls, the mountains shining with precious stones, the plains loaded with spices. These stories, tinged with the brilliant colors of their leader's rich imagination, filled the discouraged sailors with hope and good spirits.

But as they passed over the trackless ocean, and saw day by day the great billows rolling between them and the mysterious horizon, the sailors were again filled with dread. They lacked the courage to sail onward into the unknown distance. The compass began to vacillate, and no longer pointed toward the north; this confused both Columbus and his pilots. The men fell into a panic, but the resolute and patient admiral encouraged them once more. So buoyed up by his faith and hope, they continued to sail onward over the pathless waters.

The next day a heron and a tropical bird flew about the masts of the ships, and these seemed to the wondering sailors as two witnesses come to confirm the reasoning of Columbus.

At eve and morning the distant waning clouds, like those that gather round the mountaintops, took the form of cliffs and hills skirting the horizon. The cry of "land" was on the tip of every tongue. Columbus by his reckoning knew that they must still be far from any land. But fearing to discourage his men he kept his thoughts to himself, for he found no trustworthy friend among his companions whose heart was firm enough to bear his secret.

During the long passage Columbus conversed with his own thoughts, with the stars, and with God, whom he felt was his protector. He occupied his days in making notes of what he observed. The nights he passed on deck with his pilots, studying the stars and watching the seas. He withdrew into himself, and his thoughtful gravity impressed his companions sometimes with respect and sometimes with mistrust and awe.

Each morning the bows of the vessels plunged through the fantastic horizon which the evening mist had made the sailors mistake for a shore. They kept rolling on through the boundless and bottomless abyss. Gradually terror and discontent once more took possession of the crews. They began to imagine that the steadfast east wind that drove them westward prevailed eternally in this region, and that when the time came to sail homeward, the same wind would prevent their return. For surely their provisions and water could not hold out long enough for them to beat their way eastward over those wide waters!

Then the sailors began to murmur against the admiral and his seeming fruitless obstinacy, and they blamed themselves for obeying him, when it might mean the sacrifice of the lives of one hundred and twenty sailors.

But each time the murmurs threatened to break out into mutiny, Providence seemed to send more encouraging signs of land. And these for the time being changed the complaints to hopes. At evening little birds of the most delicate species, that build their nests in the shrubs of the garden and orchard, hovered warbling about the masts. Their delicate wings and joyous notes bore no signs of weariness or fright, as of birds swept far away to sea by a storm. These signs again aroused hope.

The green weeds on the surface of the ocean looked like waving corn before the ears are ripe. The vegetation beneath the water delighted the eyes of the sailors tired of the endless expanse of blue. But the seaweed soon became so thick that they were afraid of entangling their rudders and keels, and of remaining prisoners forever in the forests of the ocean, as ships of the northern seas are shut in by ice. Thus each joy soon turned to fear, so terrible to man is the unknown.

The wind ceased, the calms of the tropics alarmed the sailors. An immense whale was seen sleeping on the waters. They fancied there were monsters in the deep which would devour their ships. The roll of the waves drove them upon currents which they could not stem for want of wind. They imagined they were approaching the cataracts of the ocean, and that they were being hurried toward the abysses into which the deluge had poured its world of waters.

Fierce and angry faces crowded round the mast. The murmurs rose louder and louder. They talked of compelling the pilots to put about and of throwing the admiral into the sea. Columbus, to whom their looks and threats revealed these plans, defied them by his bold bearing or disconcerted them by his coolness.

Again nature came to his assistance, by giving him fresh breezes from the east, and a calm sea under his bows. Before the close of the day came the first cry of "Land ho!" from the lofty poop. All the crews, repeating this cry of safety, life, and triumph, fell on their knees on the decks, and struck up the hymn, "Glory be to God in heaven and upon earth." When it was over, all climbed as high as they could up the masts, yards, and rigging to see with their own eyes the new land that had been sighted.

But the sunrise destroyed this new hope all too quickly. The imaginary land disappeared with the morning mist, and once more the ships seemed to be sailing over a never-ending wilderness of waters.

Despair took possession of the crews. Again the cry of "Land ho!" was heard. But the sailors found as before that their hopes were but a passing cloud. Nothing wearies the heart so much as false hopes and bitter disappointments.

Loud reproaches against the admiral were heard from every quarter. Bread and water were beginning to fail. Despair changed to fury. The men decided to turn the heads of the vessels toward Europe, and to beat back against the winds that had favored the admiral, whom they intended to chain to the mast of his own vessel and to give up to the vengeance of Spain should they ever reach the port of their own country.

These complaints now became clamorous. The admiral restrained them by the calmness of his countenance. He called upon Heaven to decide between himself and the sailors. He flinched not. He offered his life as a pledge, if they would but trust and wait for three days more. He swore that, if, in the course of the third day, land was not visible on the horizon, he would yield to their wishes and steer for Europe.

The mutinous men reluctantly consented and allowed him three days of grace.

At sunrise on the second day rushes recently torn up were seen floating near the vessels. A plank hewn by an axe, a carved stick, a bough of hawthorn in blossom, and lastly a bird's nest built on a branch which the wind had broken, and full of eggs on which the parent-bird was sitting, were seen swimming past on the waters. The sailors brought on board these living witnesses of their approach to land. They were like a message from the shore, confirming the promises of Columbus.

The overjoyed and repentant mutineers fell on their knees before the admiral whom they had insulted but the day before and craved pardon for their mistrust.

As the day and night advanced, many other sights and sounds showed that land was very near. Toward day delicious and unknown perfumes borne on a soft land breeze reached the vessels, and there was heard the roar of the waves upon the reefs.

The dawn, as it spread over the sky, gradually raised the shores of an island from the waves. Its distant extremities were lost in the morning mist. As the sun rose it shone on the land ascending from a low yellow beach to the summit of hills whose dark green covering contrasted strongly with the clear blue of the heavens. The foam of the waves broke on the yellow sand, and forests of tall and unknown trees stretched away, one above another, over successive terraces of the island. Green valleys and bright clefts in the hollows afforded a half glimpse into these mysterious wilds. And thus the land of golden promises, the land of future greatness, first appeared to Christopher Columbus, the Admiral of the Ocean.

Our Heroes

PHOEBE CARY

Seeing what is right and doing it with firm resolve, despite the opinions of the crowd, is the mark of moral courage.

Here's a hand to the boy who has courage
    To do what he knows to be right;
When he falls in the way of temptation,
    He has a hard battle to fight.
Who strives against self and his comrades
    Will find a most powerful foe.
All honor to him if he conquers.
    A cheer for the boy who says "NO!"

There's many a battle fought daily
    The world knows nothing about;
There's many a brave little soldier
    Whose strength puts a legion to rout.

And he who fights sin singlehanded
    Is more of a hero, I say,
Than he who leads soldiers to battle
    And conquers by arms in the fray.

Be steadfast, my boy, when you're tempted,
    To do what you know to be right.
Stand firm by the colors of manhood,
    And you will o'ercome in the fight.
"The right," be your battle cry ever
    In waging the warfare of life,
And God, who knows who are the heroes,
    Will give you the strength for the strife.

The Pioneer Family

ALEXIS DE TOCQUEVILLE

In 1831 the French government sent a young aristocrat named Alexis de Tocqueville to the United States to study its prison system. The observant Tocqueville saw much more than jailhouses during his journey; his study of the democratic experiment unfolding in the New World resulted in his classic Democracy in America. *Less familiar to students of politics is Tocqueville's* A Fortnight In the Wilderness, *also based on his American notebooks, from which the selection below is excerpted. This wonderful portrait of a pioneer family tells us much about the legacy of our American heritage. Goethe once said that you must labor to possess what you have inherited. We must practice that labor today.*

The little bell which the pioneer takes care to hang round the necks of his cattle, that he may find them in the dense forest, announces from a great distance the approach to the clearing. Soon you hear the stroke of the axe. As you proceed, traces of destruction prove the presence of man. Lopped branches cover the road, trunks half calcined by fire, or maimed by steel, are still standing in the path. You go on, and reach a wood, which seems to have been struck with sudden death. Even in the middle of summer the withered branches look wintry. On nearer examination a deep gash is discovered round the bark of each tree, which, preventing the circulation of sap, quickly kills it. This is generally the planter's first measure. As he cannot in the first year cut down all the trees on his new property, he kills them to prevent their leaves overshadowing the Indian corn which he has sowed under their branches.

Next to this incomplete attempt at a field, the first step of civilization in the wilderness, you come suddenly upon the owner's dwelling. It stands in a plot more carefully cleared than the rest, but in which man still sustains an unequal struggle with nature. Here the trees have been cut down but not uprooted, and they still encumber with their stumps the ground that they formerly shaded. Round these withered remnants, corn, oak saplings, plants, and weeds of every kind spring pell-mell, and grow side by side in the stubborn and half-wild soil. In the center of this strong and diversified vegetation, stands the planter's log-house. Like the field round it, this rustic dwelling is evidently a new and hasty work. Its length seldom exceeds thirty feet; its width twenty, and height fifteen. The walls as well as the roof are composed of half-hewn trees; the cracks are filled up with moss and mud. As the traveler advances the scene becomes more animated. At the sound of his steps a group of children who had been rolling in the dirt jump up hastily, and fly towards the paternal roof, frightened at the sight of man, while two great half-wild dogs, with ears erect, and lengthened noses, come out of the hut and, growling, cover the retreat of their young masters.

At this moment the pioneer himself appears at his door. He casts a scrutinizing glance on the newcomer, bids his dogs go in, and himself sets immediately the example without exhibiting either uneasiness or curiosity.

On entering the loghouse the European looks around with wonder. In general there is but one window, before which sometimes hangs a muslin curtain; for here, in the absence of necessaries, you often meet with superfluities. On the hearth, made of hardened earth, a fire of resinous wood lights up the interior better than the sun. Over the rustic chimney are hung trophies of war or of the chase; a long rifle, a doeskin and eagles' feathers. On the right hangs a map of the United States, perpetually shaken by the wind which blows through the cracks of the wall. On a rough shelf near it are placed a few odd volumes, among them a Bible, the leaves and binding of which have been spoilt by the devotion of two generations, a Prayer-book, and sometimes one of Milton's poems, or Shakespeare's plays. With their backs to the wall are placed some rude seats, the product of the owner's industry; chests instead of wardrobes, agricultural tools, and specimens of the crop. In the middle of the room is an unsteady table, the legs of which, still covered with leaves, seem to have grown where they stand. Round this table the family assemble for their meals. On it is left an English china teapot, spoons, generally of wood, a few cracked cups, and some newspapers.

The appearance of the master of this dwelling is as remarkable as his abode. His sharp muscles and slender limbs show him at the first glance to be a native of New England; his make indicates that he was not born in the desert. His first years were passed in the heart of an intellectual and cultivated society. Choice impelled him to the toilsome and savage life for which he did not seem intended. But if his physical strength seems unequal to his undertaking, on his features, furrowed by care, is seated an expression of practical intelligence, and of cold and persevering energy. His step is slow and measured, his speech deliberate, and his appearance austere. Habit, and still more, pride, have given to his countenance a stoical rigidity, which was belied by his conduct. The pioneer despises (it is true) all that most violently agitates the hearts of men. His fortune or his life will never hang on the turn of a die, or the smiles of a woman. But to obtain competence he has braved exile, solitude, and the numberless ills of savage life; he has slept on the bare earth, he has exposed himself to the fever of the woods, and the Indian's tomahawk. Many years ago he took the first step. He has never gone back; perhaps twenty years hence he will still be going on without desponding or complaining. Can a man capable of such sacrifices be cold and insensible? Is he not influenced by a passion, not of the heart but of the brain, ardent, persevering, and indomitable?

His whole energies concentrated in the desire to make his fortune, the emigrant at length succeeds in making for himself an entirely independent existence, into which even his domestic affections are absorbed. He may be said to look on his wife and children only as detached parts of himself. Deprived of habitual intercourse with his equals, he has learnt to take pleasure in solitude. When you appear at the door of his lonely dwelling, the pioneer steps forward to meet you. He holds out his hand in compliance with custom, but his countenance expresses neither kindness nor joy. He speaks only to question you, to gratify his intelligence, not his heart; and as soon as he has obtained from you the news that he wanted to hear he relapses into silence. One would take him for a man who, having been all day wearied by applicants and by the noise of the world, has retired home at night to rest. If you question him in turn, he will give you in a clear manner all the information you require. He will even provide for your wants, and will watch over your safety as long as you are under his roof. But, in all that he does there is so much constraint and dryness; you perceive in him such utter indifference as to the result of your undertakings, that your gratitude cools.

Still the settler is hospitable in his own way, but there is nothing genial in his hospitality, because, while he exercises it, he seems to submit to one of the painful necessities of the wilderness. It is to him a duty of his position, not a pleasure. This unknown person is the representative of the race to which belongs the future of the New World; a restless, speculating, adventurous race, that performs coldly feats which are usually the result of passionate enthusiasm; a nation of conquerors, who endure savage life without feeling its peculiar charms, value in civilized life only its material comforts and advantages, and bury themselves in the wilds of America, provided only with an axe and a file of newspapers!

In describing the settler, one cannot forget the partner of his sufferings and perils. Look at the young woman who is sitting on the other side of the fire with her youngest child in her lap, superintending the preparations for supper. Like the emigrant, this woman is in the prime of life; she also recollects an early youth of comfort. The remains of taste are still to be observed in her dress. But time has pressed hardly upon her: in her faded features and attenuated limbs it is easy to see that life has to her been a heavy burden. And, indeed, this fragile creature has already been exposed to incredible suffering. At the very threshold of life she had to tear herself from the tender care of her mother, from the sweet fraternal ties that a young girl can never leave without tears, even when she quits her home to share the luxurious dwelling of a young husband. The wife of the settler, torn at once and forever from the cradle of her childhood, had to exchange the charms of society and of the domestic circle for the solitude of the forest. Her marriage bed was placed on the bare ground of the desert. To devote herself to austere duties, to submit to unknown privations, to enter upon an existence for which she was not fitted; such has been the employment of her best years; such have been the delights of her married life. Destitution, suffering, and lassitude have weakened her delicate frame, but have not dismayed her courage. While deep sadness is painted on her chiseled features, it is easy to descry religious resignation, peace, and a simple, quiet fortitude, enabling her to meet all the ills of life without fearing or defying them.

Round this woman crowd the half-clothed children, glowing with health, careless of the morrow, true children of the wilderness. Their mother turns on them from time to time a mingled look of sadness and of joy. Judging from their strength and her weakness, it would seem as if she had exhausted herself in giving them life, and without regretting the cost. The loghouse consists of a single room, which shelters the whole family at night; it is a little world, an ark of civilization in the midst of a green ocean. A few steps off the everlasting forest extends its shades, and solitude again reigns.

Plato on Fear

What should we fear? Socrates spoke of courage as involving a knowledge of what really is to be feared, and he viewed it as an integral part of all virtue, which consists in knowing which things are really good or evil. Furthermore, if moral evil is the only real evil, then the so-called evils that fortune and men inflict upon us, such as poverty, sickness, suffering, and even death, are not to be feared; if they are faced in the proper spirit, they cannot make us morally worse creatures.

Here, near the conclusion of Plato's dialogue Gorgias, *Socrates calmly and confidently predicts his own unjust death. The sinister trial he envisions (which actually came to pass in 399 B.C.) is not something he fears, because the evil actions of other men cannot harm him morally. There is only one thing Socrates truly fears, and that is to do injustice to others.*

S ocrates. Do not repeat the old story—that he who likes will kill me and get my money; for then I shall have to repeat the old answer, that he will be a bad man and will kill the good, and that the money will be of no use to him, but that he will wrongly use that which he wrongly took, and if wrongly, basely, and if basely, hurtfully.

Callicles. How confident you are, Socrates, that you will never come to harm! You seem to think that you are living in another country, and can never be brought into a court of justice, as you very likely may be brought by some miserable and mean person.

Then I must indeed be a fool, Callicles, if I do not know that in the Athenian state any man may suffer anything. And if I am brought to trial and incur the dangers of which you speak, he will be a villain who brings me to trial—of that I am very sure, for no good man would accuse the innocent. Nor shall I be surprised if I am put to death. Shall I tell you why I anticipate this?

By all means.

I think that I am the only or almost the only Athenian living who practices the true art of politics; I am the only politician of my time. Now, seeing that when I speak my words are not uttered with any view of gaining favor, and that I look to what is best and not to what is most pleasant, having no mind to use those arts and graces which you recommend, I shall have nothing to say in the justice court. And you might argue with me, as I was arguing with Polus: I shall be tried just as a physician would be tried in a court of little boys at the indictment of the cook. What would he reply under such circumstances, if someone were to accuse him, saying, "Oh, my boys, many evil things has this man done to you: he is the death of you, especially of the younger ones among you, cutting and burning and starving and suffocating you, until you know not what to do; he gives you the bitterest potions, and compels you to hunger and thirst. How unlike the variety of meats and sweets on which I feasted you!" What do you suppose that the physician would be able to reply when he found himself in such a predicament? If he told the truth he could only say, "All these evil things, my boys, I did for your health," and then would there not just be a clamor among a jury like that? How they would cry out!

I dare say.

Would he not be utterly at a loss for a reply?

He certainly would.

And I, too, shall be treated in the same way, as I well know, if I am brought before the court. For I shall not be able to rehearse to the people the pleasures which I have procured for them, and which, although I am not disposed to envy either the procurers or enjoyers of them, are deemed by them to be benefits and advantages. And if anyone says that I corrupt young men, and perplex their minds, or that I speak evil of old men, and use bitter words toward them, whether in private or public, it is useless for me to reply, as I truly might: "All this I do for the sake of justice, and with a view to your interest, my judges, and to nothing else." And therefore there is no saying what may happen to me.

And do you think, Socrates, that a man who is thus defenseless is in a good position?

Yes, Callicles, if he have that defense, which as you have often acknowledged he should have—if he be his own defense, and have never said or done anything wrong, either in respect of gods or men; and this has been repeatedly acknowledged by us to be the best sort of defense. And if anyone could convict me of inability to defend myself or others after this sort, I should blush for shame, whether I was convicted before many, or before a few, or by myself alone; and if I died from want of ability to do so, that would indeed grieve me. But if I died because I have no powers of flattery or rhetoric, I am very sure that you would not find me repining at death. For no man who is not an utter fool and coward is afraid of death itself, but he is afraid of doing wrong. For to go to the world below having one's soul full of injustice is the last and worst of all evils.

A Prayer at Valley Forge

TRADITIONAL

Valley Forge has become a place forever linked in the American mind with the virtues of courage, perseverance, and loyalty to cause. Some nine thousand of George Washington's troops went into camp there in the late autumn of 1777. By the time the snows of winter were gone, only six thousand remained. Here is a story of heroic resolve of ordinary men, as well as an example of how faith helped one extraordinary man lead the rest through.

During the Revolutionary War the British army seized Philadelphia, the "rebel capital" where the Congress had been meeting. They marched into the city with colors flying and bands playing, and made themselves at home for the winter. George Washington could do nothing to stop them. Once the British were in the city, the only thing he could do was see that they did not get out into the countryside to do any mischief. So he chose for his winter quarters Valley Forge, a place only a few miles from Philadelphia. There the American army could defend itself if attacked, and it could keep close watch on the British.

It would have been easier to fight many battles than to spend that winter in Valley Forge. It was December, and there was no shelter of any kind. Men and officers bravely set to work constructing huts for themselves. They built some of heavy logs, with roofs made of small trees wrapped with straw and laid side by side. Clay was spread on top of that. The windows were simply holes cut through the logs and covered with oiled paper.

Such a house was the height of luxury at Valley Forge. Most of the huts were made of piled-up sod, or fence rails held together by twisted twigs and daubed with clay. The snow sifted in at every opening, the rain dripped through even the best of the roofs, and the wind howled and roared and blew in at every crevice. There were few blankets, and many brave defenders of their country lay on the frozen ground because they had not even straw to put under their heads. Sometimes they sat up all night, crowding up to the fires to keep from freezing.

Their clothing was worse than their shelter. The whole army was in rags. Many of the men had no shirts, even more were without shoes. Wherever they walked, the snow was marked with blood. Some cut strips from their precious blankets and wound them about their feet to protect them from the freezing ground.

Food was scanty. Sometimes for several days the soldiers went without meat, and some companies went without even bread. When the word went around "no meat tonight," the soldiers groaned, but they never yielded.

Here is an entry in the diary of one of the men:

"There comes a soldier—his bare feet peep through his worn-out shoes, his legs nearly naked from the tattered remains of an only pair of stockings . . . his shirt hanging in strings . . . his face meager—his whole appearance pictures a person forsaken and discouraged. He comes, and cries with an air of wretchedness and despair . . . I am sick, my feet lame, my legs are sore, my body covered with this tormenting itch. My clothes are worn out, my constitution is broken, my former activity is exhausted by fatigue. Hunger and cold. I fail fast. I shall soon be no more."

One cold day a Quaker farmer was walking along a creek at Valley Forge when he heard the murmur of a solemn voice. Creeping in its direction, he discovered a horse tied to a sapling, but no rider.

The farmer stole nearer, following the sound of the voice. There, through a thicket, he saw a lone man, on his knees in the snow.

It was General Washington. His cheeks were wet with tears as he prayed to the Almighty for help and guidance.

The farmer quietly slipped away. When he reached home, he said to his wife, "The Americans will win their independence! George Washington will succeed!"

"What makes thee think so, Isaac?" she asked.

"I have heard him pray, Hannah, out in the woods today," he said. "If there is anyone on this earth the Lord will listen to, it is this brave commander. He will listen, Hannah. Rest assured, He will."

The Road Not Taken

ROBERT FROST

Courage does not follow rutted pathways.

Two roads diverged in a yellow wood,
And sorry I could not travel both
And be one traveler, long I stood
And looked down one as far as I could
To where it bent in the undergrowth;

Then took the other, as just as fair,
And having perhaps the better claim,
Because it was grassy and wanted wear;
Though as for that the passing there
Had worn them really about the same,

And both that morning equally lay
In leaves no step had trodden black.

Oh, I kept the first for another day!
Yet knowing how way leads on to way,
I doubted if I should ever come back.

I shall be telling this with a sigh
Somewhere ages and ages hence:
Two roads diverged in a wood, and I—
I took the one less traveled by,
And that has made all the difference.

Scylla and Charybdis

ADAPTED FROM A RETELLING
BY EDMUND CARPENTER

From The Odyssey, *here is the classic rough passage, the kind where you know there may be losses, where you gather your courage, lower your head, and push through as best you can.*

For ancient mariners there were countless terrors, both real and imagined, on the rolling seas. But none was more dreaded than a certain narrow passage of water said to be off the coast of southern Italy. It was a very treacherous strait, for there were two hideous points, one on either side, that all sailors strived to shun. These were called Scylla and Charybdis.

The first was a lofty crag, reaching even to the heavens with its sharp peak. Dark clouds always hovered about its top, and perpetual darkness rested upon its summit. So steep was its face, and so smooth, that no mortal could clamber up or down, though he might have twenty hands and feet. Midway up the face of this great cliff was a cave so high above the water no bowman, however strong, could reach it with his arrow from a passing ship.

In this cave dwelt Scylla, the hideous monster who gave her name to the crag itself. She had six long, scaly necks, and upon each neck was a frightful, barking head. Each of these six heads had three rows of sharp, greedy teeth, all set closely together. The story was that Scylla hid herself within the cave, but every so often would lean far out of the opening. The glaring eyes in her six heads would scan the waters below. No passing fish or dolphin could escape her dreadful vigilance, for when she saw one she would reach out and catch it in her claws, draw it into her cave, and devour it. Seamen were careful to avoid this crag, for if they allowed their vessel to go too near, Scylla would suddenly reach down and snatch some poor, unfortunate sailor from the deck and disappear with him into her den.

On the other side of the strait was another crag, called Charybdis. This peak was not so lofty as the other, and on its top grew a tall, fine fig tree, always covered with leaves and fruit. But at the foot of the cliff was a great gulf in the rock, down which the water was sucked with great violence, forming a tremendous whirlpool. Then suddenly the water would come boiling back out, as powerfully as it had been sucked in, tossing onto the waves the planks of old ships and skeletons of hapless sailors. So fierce were these movements of the water that, if a passing vessel should chance to go too near, it would be either drawn into the vortex and sucked down out of sight, or else it would be tossed about, thrown against the rock, and crushed and all the crew drowned.

It was on the long voyage home, after the Trojan War, that Ulysses and his crew came to this horrible strait where they must pass between Scylla and Charybdis.

When the heroes came within sight and hearing of the place they were filled with fear. The oars fell from their hands, and the blood drained from their faces. The horrid murmur of the fiends cut into their very brains. The towering rocks seemed to threaten them with disaster; the boiling surf hid, they knew, treacherous spots.

Ulysses, seeing the state of his men, went up and down the deck encouraging them and reminding them that they had pulled through greater perils together. He begged that they give him the same trust they had offered before and assured them he would lead them through if only they would exert all the strength and wit they had. In particular he cheered up the pilot who sat at the helm, and told him he must now show more firmness than other men, as he had more responsibility committed to him. Ulysses ordered him to steer away from the whirlpool, as it would surely swallow them all, and set a course by the higher rock.

The crew heard him, and nerved again by their captain's gallant bearing, took to the oars. Ulysses, in his shining armor, stood on the prow of the vessel, two gleaming javelins in his hand, on guard, lest the six-mouthed Scylla should attack them as they swept by her rock.

The whirlpool of Charybdis swirled dark and cavernous before them as the ship entered the strait. The crew saw how horribly the black throat drew into her all the whirling deep, so that even the bone-strewn sands at the bottom of the sea lay bare. Then suddenly she disgorged the troubled waters again, in a great cloud of spray, so that all about her the ocean boiled as in a kettle.

The noise of the thundering waves, the roaring of Charybdis, the barking of the hideous Scylla, the howling of the wind, all these were deafening and terrifying. But, spurred on by Ulysses, the men toiled at the sweeps and as they gradually drew away from the whirlpool, it seemed that all might yet be well.

But it was not to be. From her black den, Scylla suddenly darted out her six long necks, and before Ulysses could strike, she seized half a dozen mariners! Ulysses heard their shrieks, coming from high in the air, and saw them with their heels turned up, and their hands thrown out to him for sweet life. He could do nothing. In all his sufferings, he never had beheld a sight so full of miseries.

The remainder of the crew, terror-stricken at the fate of their companions, pulled frantically to get out of danger before the monster could make a second swoop. Angry at missing their prey, Charybdis boomed and Scylla barked. But the vessel shot through the roaring narrows and into the open sea. And the men, weary and heavy of heart, bent over their oars, and longed for rest.

The Star-Spangled Banner

ADAPTED FROM EVA MARCH TAPPAN

Many people sing the first verse of this song several times a year without knowing the context of its birth or the story of how our flag became the national symbol of perseverance through perilous times.

The year 1814 found the people of Maryland in trouble. A British fleet of some fifty ships had sailed into the Chesapeake Bay. Their cannon soon would be aimed at some town, but nobody knew which. The ships sailed up one river, came back down, and sailed up another, as if they had not decided which port would fall under their guns. All along the shores, people fired alarms and lit signal fires to let their neighbors know danger was near. The ships lingered, hesitated, then suddenly spread sails and ran to the north, up the bay.

"They will surely destroy us," thought the people of Annapolis. They crammed their household goods into wagons and carts, even into wheelbarrows, and hurried inland as fast as they could. But the ships sailed past Annapolis.

Suddenly there was no question which town they meant to attack. It was Baltimore. With forty-five thousand inhabitants, the port was the third-largest city in the country and a rich prize. To take it, however, the British fleet would have to get past Fort McHenry, which guarded Baltimore's harbor.

As the warships crept upstream toward the fort, the crews could see a gigantic flag with fifteen white stars and fifteen red and white stripes fluttering in the breeze above the ramparts. It was the work of widow Mary Young Pickersgill, a seamstress who specialized in making flags for Baltimore's merchant ships. Her own house wasn't large enough for the job of stitching the enormous banner together, so she and her thirteen-year-old daughter Caroline had worked on it in a Baltimore brewery. Now it flew as a proud, defiant symbol of an upstart country that was about to take on the most powerful nation in the world.

At 7 A.M. on the morning of September 13, the big British guns took aim at the flag and let loose a horrifying fire. They shot huge, 200-pound bombshells designed to explode on impact, scattering wreckage far and wide. Often, however, the erratic bombs blew up in midair. The shelling lasted nearly twenty-four hours. When dark fell the fleet used signal rockets, which traced fiery arcs across the night sky. It was a spectacular sight.

"If Fort McHenry can stand, the city is safe," Francis Scott Key muttered to himself, and he gazed anxiously through the smoke to see if the flag was still flying.

The Maryland lawyer had a particularly agonizing view of the battle—he watched from a little American vessel tied fast to the side of the British flagship. A friend had been seized as a prisoner by the British, and Key had gone out under a flag of truce to ask for his release. The British commander finally agreed to the request, but he had no intention of letting Key go back to the city with any information he might have picked up. "Until the battle is over, you and your boat stay here," he ordered.

Key had no choice but to wait it out, pacing the deck and hoping the fort could hold out. The firing went on. As long as daylight lasted, he could catch glimpses of the Stars and Stripes whenever the wind swayed the clouds of smoke. When night came, he could still see the banner now and then by the blaze of the cannon.

Finally the firing stopped. Key strained his eyes to see if the flag was still flying. "Could the fort have held out?" he wondered.

At last the faint gray of dawn appeared. He could see that some flag was flying, but it was too dark to tell whose. More and more eagerly he gazed. It grew lighter. A sudden breath of wind caught the banner, and it floated out on the breeze. It was no English flag. It was Mary Pickersgill's Stars and Stripes, still waving through the smoke and mist! Fort McHenry had stood, and the city was safe.

Overcome with emotion, Key took from his pocket an old letter and began scribbling on its back a few lines and phrases.

The British departed, and the little American boat sailed back to the city. Key gave a copy of the poem he had just written to his uncle, who had been helping defend the fort. His uncle sent it to a printer and had it struck off on some handbills. Before the ink was dry, the printer snatched one up and hurried to a tavern where many patriots were assembling.

"Listen to this!" he cried, waving the paper, and he read:

> *O say, can you see by the dawn's early light,*
> *What so proudly we hailed at the twilight's last gleaming,*
> *Whose broad stripes and bright stars, through the perilous fight*
> *O'er the ramparts we watch'd were so gallantly streaming?*
> *And the rockets' red glare, the bombs bursting in air,*
> *Gave proof through the night that our flag was still there.*
> *O say, does that star-spangled banner yet wave*
> *O'er the land of the free and the home of the brave?*

"Sing it! Sing it!" the whole company cried. Someone mounted a chair and sang the poem to an old tune. The song caught on at once. Halls, theaters, and houses soon rang with its strains as the British fleet disappeared over the horizon.

Frances Scott Key's words never lost their popularity, and more than a century later, in 1931, Congress designated "The Star-Spangled Banner" as our national anthem.

Acknowledgments

The editor gratefully acknowledges the endeavors of scholars and collectors such as James Baldwin, Andrew Lang, and Jesse Lyman Hurlbut, who in a past age devoted their energies to preserving some of the best of our heritage, and whose works have supplied this volume with many truly great stories.

Reasonable care has been taken to trace ownership and, when necessary, obtain permission for each selection included.